Roger Paine joined the Royal Navy as a junior rating, aged sixteen, and retired voluntarily twenty-eight years later in the rank of Commander. Since leaving the Navy he has worked in the City of London, as the bursar of a large grammar school, as secretary to the Trustees of the National Maritime Museum and as partnership administrator of a national firm of land agents. Now a full-time writer, he lives in an eighteenth-century cottage in rural Sussex.

CALL THE HANDS

A Collection of My Naval Yarns

ROGER PAINE

Book Guild Publishing
Sussex, England

First published in Great Britain in 2009 by
The Book Guild Ltd
Pavilion View
19 New Road
Brighton, BN1 1UF

Copyright © Roger Paine 2009
Second printing 2009

The right of Roger Paine to be identified as the author of this work has been asserted by him in accordance with the Copyright, Designs and Patents Act 1988.

All rights reserved. No part of this publication may be reproduced, transmitted, or stored in a retrieval system, in any form or by any means, without permission in writing from the publisher, nor be otherwise circulated in any form of binding or cover other than that in which it is published and without a similar condition being imposed on the subsequent purchaser.

Typesetting in ITC Baskerville by
Keyboard Services, Luton, Bedfordshire

Printed in Great Britain by
CPI Antony Rowe

A catalogue record for this book is available from
The British Library

ISBN 978 1 84624 318 9

*To Tessa, who was christened onboard
HMS Arethusa.*

Contents

	Foreword	ix
1	The Icing on the Cake	1
2	Colonial Service	11
3	Marks of Respect	19
4	Lincoln Junction	25
5	Honours and Awards	33
6	Dumped in Invergordon	41
7	Pomp and Circumstance	47
8	Ships' Mates	53
9	Cold War	61
10	Up Spirits!	73
11	Chilled Out	85
12	Paws for Thought	91
13	Over the Top	97
14	England Expects	101

15	Pieces of Eight	111
16	Fore!	123
17	Christmas at Sea	133
18	Tell Me About Yourself	139
19	The Ship's Wake	149

Foreword

'Call the Hands' is the Royal Navy's expression for what, in other walks of life, would be 'Reveille' or 'Wakey! Wakey!' The words are used every morning over the ship's broadcast system and are usually accompanied by the shrill piping notes of the sailor's traditional whistle, known as a boatswain's call. Together they signify it is time to get out of your bunk, or hammock, and start the working day.

The boatswain's call was, at one time, the only method of communicating orders on board ship other than by the human voice. Using various combinations of notes, trills and warbles, it can communicate many different instructions, including salutes or signals, as well as announcing the events which constitute a ship's daily routine from 'Call the Hands' through to 'Stand Easy', 'Hands to Dinner', and finishing the day with 'Pipe Down'.

1

THE ICING ON THE CAKE

It was one of those mornings when you knew that the decision to spend the majority of your life at sea had been the right one. But as such days did not come around very often, it was also a time to be savoured and remembered.

The Indian Ocean was as unruffled as turquoise silk. The sun, although it had already climbed high into the sky heralding another tropical day of relentless heat and humidity, was still pleasantly warm and shrouded in golden mist. Two miles away through the dancing haze were the smudges of the port we would soon be entering. Nearer at hand were acorn-shaped islands covered in dense emerald vegetation surrounded by ivory beaches. Behind the frigate in which I was serving two more ships of the same class were keeping accurate station on their leader. Grey-and-white paintwork glistened; the cleanest of clean White Ensigns and coloured signal flags flew briskly in the breeze created by the ships as they moved steadily through the water. Place, time, weather and the excitement of arriving somewhere new had combined to create a seafaring idyll. At least, that's how it seemed to me at the time.

On the bridge top, the most advantageous place from which to navigate the ship into its berth, officers and ratings in immaculate white tropical uniform were gathering for 'Harbour Stations'. The ship's engines seemed to notch up another revolution or two, as broken trees and other debris floated past, a sure indicator that within the hour we would be in harbour. The previous hazy outline of the shore was now beginning to take shape. Buildings, radio masts and, behind them, the tree-covered hills came into sight. This was the port of Victoria, capital of the Seychelles, and our small group of Royal Navy warships had been requested to visit to 'show the flag' in this former British colony on the occasion of Her Majesty The Queen's Birthday.

It was to be a prestigious visit and the three ships would lie alongside each other in the most prominent berth. The focus of the celebration, besides the usual official calls, sporting events and the ships open to visitors, would be a cocktail 'birthday' party due to be held across the flight decks of the three ships on the evening of our arrival. Some weeks earlier our captain had felt it would also be diplomatically appropriate to have some sort of centrepiece at the party. This would acknowledge the hospitality of the Seychelles government and, at the same time, maintain the traditions associated with Her Majesty's Birthday. We decided that this should be a large birthday cake. It would be baked on board, iced and decorated with the date and two flags, the Union flag and the Seychelles national flag, with their 'poles' crossed at the bottom to signify friendship and unity. I was the officer appointed in charge of this project.

The ships' cooks immediately set about baking a huge fruit cake in the biggest tray they could find. Completed it measured four feet by three feet and when iced looked magnificent. By good fortune, the petty officer cook in charge of our galleys was a skilled confectioner whose cake-decorating skills had been learned before joining the Navy in one of London's top hotels. When drawing out the design and colours on paper we had to seek advice from the yeoman of signals and consult his master copy of the International Code of Flags to ensure that the Seychelles flag was properly depicted. Icing was not an easy task and often required working late into the small hours when the ship was comparatively quiet and stable. Eventually our petty officer produced a cake which was a work of art, a tribute to what can be achieved with humble icing sugar and thoroughly befitting the event for which it was intended. Large iced cakes and warships, however, are not natural companions, so the precious centrepiece was wrapped in layers of greaseproof paper and lashed down on a shelf in the galley to await the day that had now dawned.

From the bridge the shape and features of the buildings ashore could now be clearly seen. Our navigator was busy taking fixes on prominent landmarks. The captain handed me his binoculars. 'If you look at that large building over there,' he said, 'you will see that it is flying a flag. Is it the same one as on your cake?' I looked through the glasses. 'It doesn't look like it, sir,' I replied, handing them back, 'but that is probably the Port Authority building and it is their own flag that is flying there, or something like that!' Once again he studied the approaching port through his binoculars. As the sun rose higher and the ship held its course more shoreside features came into view. 'There are other buildings flying the same flag too,' he said. 'I do hope you have got the right one on your cake!' I did not answer except to return his smug smile. 'But we will soon find out for certain,' he added, 'by asking the pilot as soon as he is up here.' I could now see the tiny pilot launch about 200 yards away. The captain ordered 'Stop engines' and the launch manoeuvred alongside our stern ladder. I noticed that this boat too was flying the same flag we could see on the buildings ashore but decided to say nothing.

Two minutes later the heavily moustachioed and sandal-footed Seychellois pilot had joined us on the bridge and we were once more underway.

THE ICING ON THE CAKE

After exchanging the usual pleasantries our captain asked, 'Tell me, pilot, what are those flags we can see flying from the buildings? They seem to be the same as the one on your launch.' 'That's our new national flag, captain,' he replied. 'We are very proud to fly it after the recent events.' The captain turned and gave me a look, which said as loudly as if he had shouted it, 'I told you so!' 'I think, Roger,' he added, 'it would be as well now if you went and changed that flag on your cake.' I grimaced and with sinking heart hurried below decks.

It was June 1979 and the 'recent events' to which the pilot referred were the establishment several weeks earlier of a one-party regime and the Seychelles Second Republic. This followed the bloodless coup some two years earlier when Albert René had installed himself as President and the former president, James Mancham, had fled into exile. On board we had been made aware of these changes, but confidential Foreign Office advice was that our visit should still proceed as planned, not least as it would be formal recognition of the new republic. No one had bothered to tell us, however, that the reconstituted government had taken the opportunity to change the national flag. It would now be hugely embarrassing if the cake with the 'old' national flag was displayed in the manner originally intended. If the 'birthday' party was still to be the showpiece of our visit there seemed to be only one solution. Change the flag.

CALL THE HANDS

Like many ship's cooks, our patissier petty officer was not known for displaying equanimity and calm under stress. His highly professional skills were aligned with a fiery temperament, and the cake, now completed and waiting to be unveiled in the evening, had not reached its present state without a large measure of thinly disguised abuse being directed at those who had dreamed up the idea in the first place. As I was one of them, I decided on a friendly approach.

The cook was in the galley supervising breakfast. 'All set for this evening, PO chef? We'll be tied up in half an hour,' I ventured. 'Good,' he replied, 'I'll be glad to get that f*****g cake out of the galley where it's taking up useful space.' The omens were not encouraging. 'Unfortunately,' I said trying to keep my tone light, 'there is a bit of a problem.' He laid down the very sharp knife with which he was slicing up chunks of raw steak for lunch and stared hard at me. Keeping my eyes on him, and the knife, I told him that the wrong Seychelles flag was on the cake, that it would have to be removed, and the cake redecorated with the correct flag, and all this needed to be done in the next few hours. I also added 'if possible' and 'please'.

He slammed the knife into his chopping board and slowly and deliberately said, 'Sir, you must be f*****g joking!' I assured him I was not. A torrent of 'f and c' language followed together with much arm waving and further stabs at the

THE ICING ON THE CAKE

board with his knife. Frightened breakfasters in the ship's company dining hall fled. Other cooks in the galley moved out of reach. I was expecting something like this but the ferocity of his anger and his comment that he would 'rather ditch the f*****g cake in the harbour' seemed a bit excessive. I decided to leave and return when the more pressing tasks of a first morning in harbour had been addressed.

Two hours later I went back to the galley. The petty officer had unwrapped the enormous cake with its beautifully decorated flags and was sitting morosely with a piece of paper on which the yeoman of signals had contritely drawn the correct Seychelles flag. 'Cake decoration isn't like writing on a blackboard, you know, it all takes time. You don't just wipe something off and add something else.' I expressed genuine sympathy and asked what could be done to retrieve the situation. Like all skilled craftsmen he did not really want to see his work destroyed and accepted that it was a challenge to be overcome. 'Well, we are almost out of icing sugar on board, but it's the colouring which is going to be difficult,' he said.

The newly constituted Seychelles flag was red, green, yellow, white and blue, with blue the predominant colour. He explained that he had used up his own small stock of icing colourings and there was not enough time to search in shops ashore. 'The only solution I have is to use ink,' suggested our master confectioner. He remembered he had seen this done once before, illegally, in a cookery competition and the brilliance of the colours had attracted much favourable comment. But then it was only for show in a competition. This was a real cake to be presented the following day to a children's orphanage nominated by the new president. Nevertheless, he agreed to do the re-icing if I took responsibility should anyone suffer from eating ink-contaminated cake. I took a deep breath and agreed. There seemed to be no alternative.

Red and green ink was available from the chart room, permanent blue Quink from the ship's office and yellow would have to be more or less neat butter. Bottles of ink were hastily brought to the galley and I left our craftsman still muttering under his breath as he mixed the icing sugar and butter and gently added drops of ink into his icing bags to get the correct colour and consistency.

The first of the 200 guests to the cocktail party arrived promptly at 6 p.m. The officers of the three ships in white mess kit mingled dutifully. The cake was mounted and floodlit and guarded by two sailor sentries flanked by the named lifebelts of the three ships. Guests unanimously admired the intricate, coloured icing which had gone into making the flags look so 'real'. Our captain was congratulated many times on producing such a symbolic and traditional centrepiece for Her Majesty's Birthday thousands of miles away from the United Kingdom. It was not exactly Trooping the Colour but it seemed like the next best thing.

At the end of the evening two of the President's aides took the cake and carefully placed it on the back seat of a large saloon car for delivery to the orphanage the next day. And as far as I know the cake was all safely eaten, without any ill effects. A day later we sailed for Mombasa.

2

COLONIAL SERVICE

The popular board game Trivial Pursuit used to have a question: 'Where are the Falklands? Are they located: A. Off the cost of Scotland? B. In the Caribbean? C. In the South Atlantic? D. Is it the name of a breed of dog?' Invariably it would be answered incorrectly. It took the Falklands War in 1982 to establish these remote islands firmly on the world map and to enshrine their name in British history.

At one time too there were only three ships that ever regularly visited the Falkland Islands and the British Dependent Territories in the South Atlantic. These were the *John Biscoe* and the *Bransfield* of the British Antarctic Survey and the Royal Navy's HMS *Endurance*. All painted plum red to be visible in the icy Antarctic waters. They would visit Stanley in the Falkland Islands at the beginning and end of each 'season' – October through to April of the following year – although rarely at the same time. For the crews, who had just completed either an 8,000-

mile voyage out from England or a 3,000-mile round trip into the Antarctic Circle, it was a welcome time to get ashore and back to 'civilisation', such as it then was. For the islanders, cut off from the outside world and with only a weekly air service to Argentina, the arrival of the Royal Navy's ice patrol ship (in which I was serving), was a very visible link with what remained of the British Empire.

As soon as we had dropped anchor in Stanley harbour, His Excellency the Governor of the Falkland Islands (always referred to as 'Hegfi', after the initials of his title) came onboard in full colonial uniform, including plumed ostrich feather hat, to inspect a guard of honour formed by our detachment of Royal Marines. Official calls ashore were made by our captain; the local Church of England vicar came onboard to assess the religious beliefs of his new congregation as well as to sell Falklands-motifed enamel ashtrays to supplement his meagre official stipend; a cocktail party for local dignitaries was held in the wardroom; and the officers received an invitation to dine at Government House. I was one of those invited.

Royal Navy tradition requires the senior officer always to be first out of a boat on reaching the shore. Our captain disembarked, saluted and thanked the coxswain. At the top of the steps on the jetty was the captain's official transport, with a smartly uniformed chauffeur, waiting to take him to Government House. Whilst such arrangements might have been expected it was surprising to find that 'Hegfi's' official transport in Stanley was a London taxi – one of the original sit-up-and-beg-type with an open front compartment used for luggage when travelling between London mainline stations. The 'for hire' meter flag had been discreetly covered up but in all other respects the vehicle was a genuine thirty-year-old black cab.

As there was no other means of getting to Government House, other than to walk, our captain offered myself and two others the opportunity to 'share his taxi'. I sank into the creased maroon leather seats. The chauffeur, who introduced himself as Trevor Harding as he held open the passenger door, climbed into the driver's seat, adjusted his black peaked cap and straightened his tie before finally setting off up the jetty.

Ross Road was one of Stanley's half a dozen or so properly tarmacadamed roads and ran westwards alongside the harbour until a little over a mile distant it reached the Governor's residence. This was a rambling mixture of single- and two-storey buildings with a large conservatory facing north across the harbour and an imposing flagstaff in the grounds where the Union flag was to be famously rehoisted by the Royal Marines after the recapture of Stanley in June 1982.

We drew up at the white wooden gate, which

opened onto a gravel pathway which led to the main entrance. Our chauffeur held open the taxi door and asked if we would walk up to the front door and ring the bell whilst he went around to the rear to park. We crunched up the drive, entered the small glass-fronted vestibule and pressed the polished brass bell. It echoed through the house but nothing happened. We looked at each other and wondered whether we should ring again. However, as this was a personal invitation from the Governor it seemed unlikely that he and his wife had forgotten there would be guests arriving. We decided to wait. Several minutes later the door was opened by a smart manservant with neatly brushed hair, a white starched jacket, black trousers and tie. He smiled politely. 'Good evening, gentlemen. Please come in. His Excellency is expecting you.' The butler, as we assumed he was, held open the door and we went inside.

I sensed immediately there was something vaguely familiar about the Governor's butler and then realised that it was none other than Trevor Harding, our recent chauffeur in the taxi. He must have parked, run into the house, exchanged his black jacket for a white one, combed his hair, and with driving responsibilities temporarily suspended, was now responsible for overseeing the smooth running of the dinner. We gathered in the drawing room, where we were joined by the officers who had walked from the jetty, local officials and by 'Hegfi' and his wife. Our ever-attentive butler, Trevor, served glasses of sherry from a decanter on a silver tray and promptly at 8 p.m. announced, 'Dinner is served.'

Twelve of us sat down to dinner in the chintz-wallpapered dining room and soup was served. I heard a voice asking if I would like a glass of wine. I turned my head to reply and immediately recognised the waiter. Once again it was Trevor Harding, our ex-chauffeur and ex-butler! This ubiquitous factotum with the chameleon-like ability to change and appear in whatever domestic role was required had now removed his white jacket, replaced his conventional tie with a black bow tie, and was now waiting at table. 'Yes, please,' I replied, smiling as if at an old friend, adding, 'Hello again!' But Mr Harding, who clearly had been trained not to display any form of familiarity, despite our obvious mutual recognition, only nodded and filled my glass.

Roast mutton for the main course was inevitable and Trevor's waiting at table was impeccable. We stood for the loyal toast, coffee was served, and several cigars were smoked. Shortly before midnight the Governor announced that his car was waiting outside so we shook hands and I watched from the hallway as our captain stepped into the London taxi with the door held dutifully open by Trevor Harding, back once again in his peaked black cap and double-breasted jacket.

The following spring we sailed into Stanley for

the final time. As the Governor was shortly due to complete his five-year tour, and as we had space in our forward hold, it had been agreed that HMS *Endurance* would be the cheapest and quickest means of transporting 'Hegfi's' London taxi back to the United Kingdom. We loaded the vehicle, lashed it down with chains, covered it with a hatch tarpaulin and headed north via Buenos Aires and Madeira.

On arrival in Portsmouth we waited for customs officers to board. Our request for customs clearance had included 'one London taxi', which had initially been regarded by HM Customs and Excise as an RN leg-pull. It was, of course, no hoax. I had been given responsibility for the vehicle, now uncovered and with Stanley mud still on the wheels. I waited whilst the customs officer carried out a thorough inspection. 'What had the vehicle been used for?' 'To transport the Governor on duty.' The official looked sceptical. 'Who was the driver?' 'The Governor had his own chauffeur.' I did not think it necessary to mention his other roles. Chassis number and engine number were checked against export records. 'The mileage since leaving the United Kingdom,' the inspector said, looking at me intently, 'appears to show that this taxi has only done 465 miles in five years. I find that difficult to believe.' I replied that such mileage seemed rather high to me when, as I explained, there were only about three miles of roads in Stanley the Governor would ever be likely to use. The look of complete disbelief remained but, as he was unable to prove otherwise, clearance was granted.

A dockyard crane hoisted the veteran London taxi out of the ship. Although I cannot be certain that it was Trevor Harding who was the crane driver, I like to imagine that if the Governor's chauffeur, butler and waiter had also been employed in this role he might have raised his hand in a sad farewell.

In the middle of a busy naval dockyard, as the taxi was swallowed up into the back of a waiting lorry, it looked forlorn, shorn of its last remaining dignity. I watched as the vehicle drove away and disappeared. With it, I sensed, went a tiny fragment of the British Empire, as symbolic as the removal of one more pink speck from a world map.

3

MARKS OF RESPECT

The Royal Navy has many traditions. One that endures is that of stopping a warship at sea in the position where sea battles were fought or ships were sunk, as a mark of respect for the sailors who were killed or drowned there.

Position 36.11N 6.23W. In 1958 when HMS *Victorious* sailed for the Mediterranean after ten years of modernisation, she was the most advanced aircraft carrier in the Royal Navy. As a young sailor in my first ship I was proud to be serving in this huge vessel and thrilled by the prospect of going ashore for the first time in Gibraltar. It was early October and the warmth of the sun was in stark contrast to the chill autumn days we had left behind in Portsmouth.

The coastline of Spain was clearly visible, but now we sailed to within three miles where the bright sunshine reflecting off the sea made the lighthouse on the cliffs seem unnaturally close. It was Cape Trafalgar. One hundred and fifty-three years previously these same seas had witnessed the defeat of the combined fleets of France and Spain by the British fleet under Admiral Lord Nelson.

It was late afternoon and on the quarterdeck I was close to the sea as it splashed over the immaculately scrubbed decks. The ship's engines had been stopped and for a warship with fifteen hundred men on board it was eerily silent. The ship rolled in the broad Atlantic swell and the chaplain conducted a brief service in memory of the 429 British and 2,800 French and Spanish sailors killed in the Battle of Trafalgar on 21 October 1805. Our captain read aloud Nelson's prayer, which he composed on the eve of the battle: 'May the Great God, whom I worship, grant to my Country, and for the benefit of Europe in general, a great and glorious Victory...' We sang 'Eternal Father, Strong to Save' and the chaplain threw into the sea a wreath of laurel leaves. As it slowly floated away we observed a minute's silence.

Suddenly I was able to visualise the lines of wooden ships with their canvas sails billowing and signal flags streaming, sailing towards each other, and to imagine the fear the sailors in both fleets must have experienced as their vessels fired broadside after broadside at point-blank range. I watched as the wreath began to sink down to where the hulks of the ships lay, tombs for the remains of those brave nineteenth-century sailors

MARKS OF RESPECT

destined to never again see the ports from which they had so gallantly sailed.

Position 3.33N 104.28E. After guardship duty in Hong Kong and shore leave in Subic Bay in the Philippines, amongst the United States Navy on 'R & R' from the Vietnam War in 1972, it was refreshing to be back at sea. I was now an officer in the frigate HMS *Lincoln* on passage to Singapore through the South China Sea. Just over the horizon lay the coast of Malaysia and the surrounding sea was busy with ocean freighters and tankers. At noon we slowed almost to a stop but remained in the shipping lane.

Thirty-one years previously on a similarly clear, sunny day, Vice Admiral Sir Tom Phillips in the battleship HMS *Prince of Wales*, accompanied by the battle cruiser HMS *Repulse*, was returning to Singapore having failed to find the expected invasion by Japanese forces on the Malaysian coast. At eleven o'clock in the morning on 10 December 1941 both ships were suddenly attacked by bombs and torpedoes dropped from enemy aircraft launched from shore bases already held by the Japanese. The ships were sunk within an hour of each other with the combined loss of 840 men.

The breeze created by our movement through the translucent sea had ceased and we stood in stifling heat on the open quarterdeck. The propellers continued to turn idly to create a soapsuds-like wash. The heat from the deck came up through our sandals and perspiration soaked our white tropical uniforms. The captain read the naval prayer 'O Eternal Lord God who alone spreadest out the Heavens...' and the master-at-arms threw a Chinese-made wreath of artificial flowers over the stern. As it churned away in our wake and we continued on our voyage to Singapore, I remembered the two ships and their sailors lying in their eternal grave 250 feet below who had never been able to complete the same journey.

Position 31.8S 45.26W. On Remembrance Day at sea a traditional church service is always held. In 1982 I was serving on an admiral's staff taking the first group of ships to the South Atlantic after the Falklands conflict earlier that same year. HMS *Antrim*, our flagship, had been involved in the campaign. At 11 a.m. on Sunday 14 November we gathered on the flight deck for our service. We were 600 miles from the coast of Brazil and over 1,000 miles from the Falkland Islands.

It was nearly midsummer in the southern hemisphere but there were heavy grey clouds and the ship, although stopped, rolled clumsily in the deep blue-black troughs and breaking white crests of the ocean which surges incessantly between the subcontinents.

Remembrance services can sometimes seem remote from the wars which they commemorate.

MARKS OF RESPECT

Not on this occasion. The very recent conflict and the loss of 252 British servicemen was uppermost in our minds, and everyone felt a sense of personal loss. When the evocative words 'When you go home, tell them of us and say, For your tomorrows, these gave their today' were said, followed by two minutes' silence, the poignancy of the occasion raised the hairs on the back of my neck and probably moistened many eyes.

Wreaths of poppies were thrown into the sea. As they drifted away in the ship's wake an albatross, a frequent follower of ships across the vast distances of the southern oceans, glided above on its graceful wings keeping pace as the ship rose and dipped with the waves. I looked up and watched its almost motionless flight and wondered whether it was too fanciful to imagine that this majestic bird, which legend says retains the souls of drowned mariners, was visiting on this day of remembrance to pay its own timely mark of respect.

4

LINCOLN JUNCTION

A 'run ashore' the night before going to sea the following day is very much part of a seafarer's life. The last opportunity to down a pint, swallow a tot or two, or even sink a skinful, prior to spending weeks or months at sea, is a tradition which has survived over the centuries.

It was late September 1973. For the second consecutive year Iceland was taking unilateral action to prevent British trawlers from fishing their traditional waters off the Icelandic coast. Whilst arguments over the legality of extending territorial waters to 200 miles were taking place at the European Commission in Brussels, a different type of battle was being fought at sea.

The Icelandic government deployed its gunboats to harass British trawlers and, whenever possible, to destroy their nets and lines, worth hundreds of thousands of pounds. The British government, in order to prevent this happening, would despatch a Royal Navy frigate – sometimes two – to protect the trawlermen. The 'Cod

Wars', as they become known, were headline news.

I was serving in the frigate HMS *Lincoln* and we had, on two separate occasions earlier that year, been in action in the icy northern waters. In July relations between the two countries had reached a particularly serious state when our ship had been deliberately rammed by the Icelandic gunboat *Aegir*, whose captain had already earned the nickname 'Mad Axeman' in view of his determination to cut trawlers' fishing lines with no regard for the safety of the ships and their crews. Reckless manoeuvres such as we had experienced might have been legitimate on dodgem cars at a funfair but it was extremely dangerous when two warships were steaming in close proximity in the North Atlantic.

As soon as the damage had been repaired in Chatham Dockyard our ship was ready for another patrol. However, as the International Regulations for Preventing Collisions at Sea appeared to count for little in encounters with Icelandic gunboats, we felt that something had to be done to prevent the potentially serious consequences of being rammed again. On the evening before we sailed we went for a final 'run ashore' to our favourite pub in Rochester and debated, over several pints of Shepherd Neame beer, how this might best be achieved.

After closing time we walked back to our ship through the dimly lit dockyard still discussing the matter, laughing, joking and singing a few bawdy choruses. HMS *Lincoln* was a happy ship – the result of two years in commission, crossing-the-line ceremonies, on-board pantomimes and 'Sods Operas'. So when one of our party, having attended an urgent call of nature behind some corrugated-iron sheds, returned to announce he had solved the problem of being rammed by Icelandic gunboats, it was not surprising that he should be greeted by howls of derisive laughter.

Behind the sheds, rusting among the weeds, were a pile of old railway lines, probably dumped there when no longer required by dockyard trains or trams. The disused lines were about 150 feet long and it was these, he suggested, that could be welded onto our ship so they stuck out like giant spines over our stern to force 'Mad Axeman' and his fellow gunboat skippers to keep their distance.

At first the idea seemed too far-fetched but with caution long since removed by Messrs Shepherd and Neame, and as we were sailing in eight hours' time, three of us picked up one length of railway line while another three picked up a second. To choruses of 'Heigh-ho! Heigh-ho!' we marched back to the ship with our new-found defensive weapons. The two lines were left on the jetty overnight with instructions to our shipwright to reduce each one by about thirty feet. They were then carried on board, where our captain declared himself delighted to have such original additional protection.

CALL THE HANDS

We sailed on schedule, and as soon as we were into the River Medway the two railway lines were securely lashed down with rope and wire on both sides of our quarterdeck, so that about fifty feet protruded over the stern; time did not allow them to be welded to our superstructure. Despite the vibration and the ship's pitching movement the lines were extremely steady and solid and instilled a sense of confidence throughout the ship. The next day the *Daily Telegraph* featured an aerial photograph of HMS *Lincoln* with the amusing caption, 'HMS *Porcupine* Goes to War'!

At the end of our patrol, during which we suffered more damage from deliberate ramming by Icelandic gunboats on our port and starboard sides but, thanks to our railway lines, none to our stern, we sailed back to Chatham. Although the spines were strictly unofficial and doubtless in breach of Queen's Regulations, it was decided that they should remain in place until we were alongside in the dockyard.

Like any RN ship returning from sea we had to look our best for entering harbour and this would mean painting our rails which, after sixteen days of sea and salt, were a great deal more rusty and grimy than when originally fitted. So how were they to be painted? Someone suggested it should be done as a competition with one officer and one rating painting a rail each, with a case of beer as the prize for the one who completed the job in the shortest time. As I was

LINCOLN JUNCTION

the officer who remarked 'I don't mind having a go!', I was immediately selected.

Twenty-four hours before we arrived in our home port the ship was slowed sufficiently to give a reasonably firm platform on which to undertake the challenge. Officers and ratings gathered on vantage points around the ship's quarterdeck to cheer on the contestants. With a lifebelt and a lifeline, I and a sailor climbed over the stern rails and sat with legs astride our respective railway lines. Mine was the port rail. On the blast of a whistle from the first lieutenant, who was acting as umpire, we slithered ourselves awkwardly out to the end of the rails. With fifty feet of rusting steel between my legs, the vibration from the ship's propellers in the sea fifteen feet below, and the springy tension of the rails as they bounced up and down in the North Sea swell, made me fervently wish I had never been so naive as to open my mouth.

My companion painter and I reached the end of our rails at the same time. The spring here was even more marked and it was necessary to grip the narrow rail tightly with my inner thighs as I reached out to hang the paint pot over the end. The intention was that we should both then slide our way backwards painting the rail beneath us as we went. Our paint pots were full of the ship's own red paint rather than the RN's standard grey. It was a long-held tradition that HMS *Lincoln* always had red upper-deck beading, so the spines would have to match. Each of us had a two-inch paintbrush.

The umpire again blew his whistle. The race was on! The sailors who had been laying bets on who might finish first spontaneously burst into song:

> *Now the sultan said to Aladdin, my palace you must paint,*
> *But Aladdin like a big OD said 'No, I f*****g ain't!',*
> *So he grabbed himself a two-inch brush and a pot of black enamel,*
> *And shoved it up the a******e of the sultan's favourite camel!*

This crude chorus carried out to us as we perched above the waves. Although appropriately amusing encouragement in the circumstances, I was in no mood for joining in.

Hanging on to the spine with one hand, whilst painting with the other, and all the time edging myself backwards on the bouncing rail was not easy. Then the inevitable happened. I dropped my paintbrush into the sea. A huge cheer went up from the watching sailors who realised that, barring a similar mishap, my fellow painter would be the easy winner. Marooned on a steel railway line which was fixed to a warship in the North Sea with only a pot of red paint and my lifebelt, I felt a total fool!

LINCOLN JUNCTION

Determined, however, to complete the challenge I shouted for a replacement brush and scraped and slid my way back along the rail as quickly as I could. Armed again with a new brush I once more had to slither nearly forty feet out to where my painting had been so cruelly interrupted. The sailor painting the starboard rail was now halfway through his task and, by the time I clambered back on board more than five minutes after him, the case of beer was already being shared around.

When we arrived in Chatham there was as much media attention on our innovative protection, now gleaming in its new red coat of paint, as there was on the damage inflicted by the Icelandic gunboats. In recognition of our unusual armour's original use, the ship's crew had also hung over the stern a large painted sign with the words 'LINCOLN JUNCTION' in the shape of the London Underground logo!

On this humorous note our participation in the 'Cod Wars' for that year came to an end. But it was not so amusing for myself. For I had to explain to my wife how it was that, after nearly three weeks at sea off Iceland, I had returned home with my inner thighs looking like raw meat where the skin had been totally rubbed away as a result of sliding along a railway line! Not only was this wholly unbelievable but also so excruciatingly painful that normal marital relations had to be temporarily postponed.

5

HONOURS AND AWARDS

'Where is Zamboanga?' asked a voice from the darkness. I had only been on watch for ten minutes and was busy at the chart table at the rear of the bridge, checking our course to ensure that we arrived off Lantao Island in good time for our arrival in Hong Kong at precisely 10 a.m. Again the question came out of the darkness. This time a certain testiness identified the voice of my captain. I had not heard him come onto the bridge, climb into his chair and with the aid of a torch begin to read the latest signals.

With the name 'Zamboanga' hanging in the air and my eyes only slowing becoming accustomed to the inky blackness, the situation seemed almost surreal. 'Zamboanga,' he repeated, 'where is it?' 'Haven't a clue, sir. Why?' 'Well, you'd better find out sharpish,' snapped the hunched figure, 'because we've been told to go there next month!' 'Whatever for?' I asked. 'I have no idea,' he retorted, 'except the Commander-in-Chief says we must, so we must.' He resumed reading.

I checked our course again, told the operations room to keep an extra watch for increased small craft traffic as we approached the outer islands and went to the chartroom to discover the exact location of Zamboanga. The name did not sound real and over the course of the next few weeks, and for years afterwards, I never met anyone who had heard of it either. But I soon found out that it did exist and I was ashamed of my ignorance at not recognising one of the major cities in the Philippines. It is also the ancient capital of Mindanao and, like much of the southern Philippines, is traditionally Muslim, in contrast to the American-influenced, and Catholic, north.

I learned later that we had been asked to visit at the specific request of the Philippines government in official recognition of the valuable assistance the ship had provided in the wake of a typhoon which had swept through the islands two months earlier. I also discovered that no RN ship had visited Zamboanga for thirty years and our visit would only be for four days owing to 'civil unrest ashore'. We were assured, however, that this would have no effect on the important nature of our visit.

The passage south across the Sulu Sea was uneventful and a hazy tropical morning greeted our arrival off the headland of the narrow channel that led up through low-lying islands to the city of Zamboanga. We embarked the pilot and the naval attaché who had flown down from Manila. The latter was tired and dishevelled after a typically frustrating Philippines journey and was clearly unsettled by the unknown diplomatic territory he was about to enter. There was already a nagging feeling that this visit would not be quite the 'reward' to the representatives of Her Majesty's Government that was intended.

This was reinforced on arrival when we were told that the civil unrest ashore had now escalated to a state of martial law being imposed on Zamboanga and the surrounding area. We also learned that the militia garrisoned in the city did not see eye to eye with the regional government and they, in turn, would have no dealings with the central government. This made it extremely difficult for us, as visitors, to appreciate local political sensitivities that were also exacerbated by the religious differences that had polarised the community for centuries. Local officials clearly had more important matters to occupy their minds than extending a welcome to the Royal Navy.

On the final morning of our visit I was officer of the day on the gangway before we were due to sail. The ship's berth was alongside the city's central square and provided a grandstand view of the local population attempting to go about their business whilst threatened with imminent civil war. But Philippinos are permanently cheerful and optimistic and the presence of a British ship with smart, friendly sailors, one of whom was armed and stood at the bottom of the gangway, represented a semblance of stability in a volatile environment. Suddenly the sound of gunfire, squealing tyres and over-revved engines shattered this illusion.

Three large 4x4 jeepneys, painted in dazzling rainbow colours, came to an abrupt halt in a cloud of dust at the bottom of our gangway. A group of long-haired figures clad in camouflage combat fatigues jumped to the ground and suddenly there were twenty-five heavily armed men on the jetty threatening the ship. Their leader and his closest followers rushed up the gangway. Our armed sentry's role was about as useful as the lifebuoy on its stand next to him.

With my telescope under my arm, and only the quartermaster and the boatswain's mate to provide assistance, I felt exceedingly vulnerable. My 'Good morning, welcome aboard...' disappeared in a bear hug from a strong, wiry man with thick black moustache, colourful bandana and a very large revolver strapped to his waist. I fleetingly imagined that the ship was about to be taken over by terrorists, but such fears were dispelled by the genuine smiles, handshakes and embraces that were extended to myself and the two sailors.

'We come to see your *capitano*! I am the *generalissimo* commanding the town and these are my officers,' announced the moustachioed leader, laughing. His aides smiled and laughed too, fingering their bandoliers of ammunition that crossed their chests and brandishing their rifles. In such circumstances, and whatever their motive, it was not a request I could refuse. I told the boatswain's mate to inform the captain he could expect some guests in his cabin in approximately two minutes. 'We bring you something verree, verree special,' added the general and pointed to a cardboard shoebox held by his bearded second in command.

'Follow me, please,' I said and led the way along the upper deck. I was followed by the general and two officers while the other stayed on guard at the top of the gangway. The remainder of his troops lounged on the jetty alongside their jeepneys, cleaning their guns, laughing and smoking. The early-morning sun, the bustle of traders and packed buses heralded the start of another normal day in Zamboanga. Except on board Her Majesty's frigate.

I knocked on the captain's cabin door and entered, followed by our visitors, who without waiting for formal introductions, embraced the captain with face-to-face contact and hearty thumps on his back. Whether bristling moustaches and sweaty camouflage jackets being pressed against his freshly shaved face and immaculate white shirt was quite what he had expected, I never found out. But as the person responsible for allowing these guests on board I felt it my duty to remain. With five men, three of whom were heavily armed and festooned with ammunition pouches and guns, the small cabin suddenly seemed extremely full.

With due ceremony the cardboard box was placed on the captain's desk. After a few words of introduction the *generalissimo* explained in broken English: 'We come from President Marcos to award you and your crew the Philippines Civil Medal for your work in relief of the floods.' This was followed by another handshake and embrace. The captain was then invited to open the box. My initial suspicion that it was a shoebox was confirmed by the words 'Freeman, Hardy & Willis' stamped on one end. What exactly a British shoe retailer's box was doing in a strife-torn Philippino island at least 10,000 miles from where it was manufactured only added another twist to an already bizarre situation. The captain leaned forward and lifted the lid. The white-toothed grins of pleasure from the soldiers were expectant as he drew out a handful of dark- and light-blue pieces of plastic with safety pins attached to the back. 'One for each of your men!' enthused the general and for a moment I thought he was about to draw his pistol and fire it into the air in celebration. The damage a bullet might have done in such a confined space did not bear contemplation.

A more appropriate celebration, the captain decided, was a drink. To the delight of our guests he poured large brandies and we drank toasts to each other, to flood relief and to *El Presidente*. The general was into his second brandy, the first having been swallowed at a gulp, when a frantic knocking at the door revealed a fearsome-looking *soldado*. A flurry of excited exchanges in Spanish followed, the captain and I had our arms pumped again and the general and his officers left the ship as swiftly as they had arrived. At the bottom of the gangway the donor of the Philippines Civil Medal turned, saluted elaborately and jumped into his waiting jeepney. The safe return of their leader excited the soldiers and as the open-topped vehicles sped away two rounds of automatic fire ripped into the morning air. As soon as the dust settled and daily life in Zamboanga had resumed we decided our visit was definitely over and within an hour were heading downriver for the open sea.

But what should we do with the medals? The sudden award of a medal generated much excitement and everyone eagerly looked forward to wearing their Philippines Civil Medal and possibly adding the letters 'PCM' after their names. Although it was reluctantly acknowledged that very little prestige could be attached to a piece of coloured plastic which might have looked more at home on a Woolworths button counter. Nevertheless, it was a medal awarded by a foreign government and proper procedures had to be followed.

Queens Regulations Appendix J28 Part 2 entitled 'Regulations concerning the acceptance and wearing by persons in the service of the Crown of orders, decorations and medals conferred by heads of governments of foreign states and by members of the commonwealth overseas of which the Queen is not the head of state' appeared to cover our situation to the letter.

On this basis a request for permission to wear the PCM was signalled to London. The Ministry of Defence offered congratulations and respectfully forwarded our request to Her Majesty The Queen for formal approval. A month passed before a message arrived to announce that 'Her Majesty very much regrets that the wearing of the Philippines Civil Medal is not permitted and the insignia may not be worn...'

It was a bitter blow to learn that the contents of the Freeman, Hardy & Willis shoebox were officially regarded as worthless. In spite of not having the royal seal of approval the medals which had been brought aboard with such ceremony, and presented with such bravado, were placed on the counter of the ship's canteen and those who wanted a PCM helped themselves.

For the next few months the blue plastic ribbon was worn with dented pride on working overalls, shirts and hats. Although it was never a real 'Honour', or an 'Award', it had to be the next best thing!

6

DUMPED IN INVERGORDON

Scotland has a long association with the Royal Navy. From the naval dockyard at Rosyth on the east coast to the submarine base at Helensburgh on the west. There has also been a time-honoured tradition of the Navy using the seas around Scotland for operational training.

But when a malfunctioning torpedo lands on a beach on the Kyle of Lochalsh, or sheep are traumatised by a misdirected 4.5-inch shell fired onto to the Hebridean ranges, the Navy makes headlines for the wrong reasons. To appease any embarrassment such incidents could cause, and to express thanks for the use of Scottish waters by warships, above and below the sea, it used to be customary to send a frigate on an annual 'goodwill tour' to dispense traditional naval hospitality around the Scottish coastline.

In 1978 I was serving in the ship selected for this duty. One of the ports we visited was Invergordon. No longer the distinguished anchorage for Grand Fleet battleships it had once been but more a busy oil-rig servicing port north of Inverness. On the day of arrival our first function was the captain's buffet lunch party on the bridge. As a host officer I was ready at 12.30 p.m. to meet the guests. Led by a midshipman from the gangway three decks below, a distinguished-looking couple came onto the bridge. A steward offered drinks from a silver tray and whilst the captain chatted to the gentleman I made conversation with the lady. Dressed in a checked tweed suit, matching hat with a feather and sensible brown lace-up brogue shoes, she was the epitome of a Scottish country gentlewoman.

Somewhat out of breath, having climbed several steep ladders, she took a large sip of gin and tonic and exclaimed, 'What-a thump!' She had a strong nasal inflection in her voice which made her lisp. 'What-a thump!' she repeated. Not fully understanding what she was saying but assuming this statement referred to the view we had of the town of Invergordon through the bridge windows, and not wishing to appear impolite, I thought it best to agree. 'Yes,' I replied, 'Invergordon is a dump. It was a dump when I first came here and still looks pretty much a dump now.'

'I didn't say what-a dump,' she retorted angrily. 'I said what-a thump! What-a thump it was from the jetty onto the gangway!' I then realised, to my horror, that 'thump' was a distortion, due to her lisp, of the word 'jump' and she was complaining about the extremely steep angle of the gangway onto the jetty which had forced her to jump before she came on board. I had also been completely misguided in my assumption that when saying 'What-a thump!' she had been referring to her native town as a dump. I offered abject apologies but to no avail. 'It's no good, you thaid Invergordon's a dump!' she insisted, fixing me with a glassy stare. Then, to my complete amazement, she continued, 'But you're right, y'know. Invergordon is a dump, I agree-th with you!'

Now even more confused, I apologised again. But greatly amused at the turn of events she decided others should know. She called across the bridge to her husband. 'Darlink,' she hooted, 'there's-an officer here who thays Invergordon's a dump!' 'What's that?' replied the Lord Lieutenant of Ross and Cromarty, who I had been told he was. 'What did you say, m'dear?' Obviously he was hard of hearing so she felt compelled to shout. 'I said, darlink, there's-an officer here who thays Invergordon's a dump! And I agree-th with him!' She laughed heartily and finished her drink.

Her distinctive voice caused everyone to stop talking and stare in our direction. The captain glared furiously at me. 'Did you really say Invergordon was a dump, Roger?' 'Well, er, yessir, but I was only, er, agreeing with what I thought this lady was, er, saying. I hadn't realised...' My voice tailed limply away. 'Extraordinary!' he growled. 'On behalf of this officer' – he stared pointedly in my direction – 'I apologise to all my guests!'

Conversation resumed and lunch was served. Nevertheless, my guest continued to enjoy the apparent aptness of my remark by muttering happily to herself, 'He's right. Invergordon is a dump!' The captain, needless to add, did not share her amusement and later when the guests had departed demanded a full explanation of 'my woefully rude behaviour'. My reasons, however, were brushed aside and I felt thoroughly chastened.

The ship's official cocktail party was held the same evening. This was for a larger number of guests but would include the VIPs who had attended the lunch. Once again I was a host officer. The guests streamed over the gangway which, thanks to the ebbing tide, was no longer at such an acute angle and the cause of the misinterpreted 'thump' six hours earlier.

Suddenly the evening air was shattered by an excited shriek which I immediately recognised. 'There he is'th! There he is'th! There's-a the officer who thaid Invergordon's a dump! And he's right! It is a dump!' The Lord Lieutenant's wife hurried to where I was standing, kissed me on both cheeks and proclaimed me a hero. Fortunately the noise of conversation, clinking glasses and the chortles of her lady friends saved any words from reaching my captain's ears. Although throughout the party she insisted on introducing me as 'the officer who called Invergordon a dump'.

As an ambassador for the Royal Navy in Scotland it was to my great relief when we slipped quietly down the Cromarty Firth at first light the following morning.

7

POMP AND CIRCUMSTANCE

Throughout the 1970s and 1980s many of Britain's former colonies disappeared from the world map. It was as if a schoolteacher had wiped the colour pink from the blackboard after an old-fashioned geography lesson.

In November 1981 it was the turn of Antigua and Barbuda in the Caribbean to become one independent nation state. The Royal Navy, represented by HMS *London* with an admiral embarked, was ordered to be present for the last rites. The event was also honoured by the presence of Princess Margaret, en route to her favourite holiday island of Mustique. Serving on the admiral's staff I was involved with the protocol for the RN's role in the independence ceremonies. But no amount of careful planning can ever ensure that everything happens as intended. And so it proved.

The Union flag was hauled down for the last time at an evening ceremony held on Antigua's tiny cricket ground where, after two days of torrential rain, a Royal Marines band in traditional white pith helmets squelched bravely through the mud playing 'Rule, Britannia!' and 'What Shall We Do With The Drunken Sailor?' To conclude the celebrations a dinner was held on board the flagship in honour of the royal visit.

A reconnaissance visit had been made by Princess Margaret's private secretary. His duties included fixing a strategically placed steel hook to the dining table for the royal handbag containing her much-loved cigarettes, and ensuring that an upright grand piano was available 'in case HRH wants to tinkle the ivories after you've passed the port.' The first had been easier to accommodate than the second which, with great difficulty, had to be manoeuvred up into the admiral's dining cabin from the petty officers' mess three decks below.

Princess Margaret, the British High Commissioner and the new Prime Minister were half an hour behind schedule in arriving at the ship. I was asked to telephone Government House to enquire when they could be expected. 'When the rain stops' came the less-than-helpful reply. 'Can you tell me,' I asked, 'when that will be?' 'In ten minutes!' came the answer. This forecast, which was apparently based on intimate local knowledge, proved uncannily accurate and the royal party duly arrived as predicted.

The dinner was preceded by a reception. The gold-laced white uniforms and the colourful dresses of the ladies, including Princess Margaret in salmon pink, made a glittering sight in the narrow confines of the ship's wardroom. The atmosphere was relaxed until the young steward, who had been ordered to attend to HRH's legendary liquid refreshment needs, politely enquired 'Water, ma'am?' as he handed her another tumbler full of Scotch, only to be rebuffed with a direct stare and the unanswerable question, 'Why?'

A quartet of Royal Marines musicians, having removed their muddy boots and exchanged brass for strings, played suitable selections. The dining table, with the ship's silver, menu cards adorned with the newly independent state's flag of a golden sun, symbolising the dawn of a new era, and linen table napkins entwined with 'HMS LONDON' sailors' cap ribbons, looked magnificent. Immediately Princess Margaret removed her ribbon and requested the admiral to tie it around her neck as a silk choker. With her diamond necklace and earrings it was a charming personal gesture which brought a ripple of polite applause from the seated diners. Iced tomato rings, roast quail in nests and raspberries in brandy cups was served and a traditional British dinner, redolent of grand colonial houses in the tropics, provided an appropriate contrast to the formalities which had heralded the island's independence two hours earlier.

At the end of the dinner the ladies retired

before the port was served. Minutes later I was summoned by the admiral's wife. 'Quickly!' she said. 'HRH is in the admiral's loo, but there doesn't seem to be any water with which to flush it!' An occurrence, not unknown, in many ships. I hurried to the wardroom where the ship's officers were in the bar holding their own independence party. I approached the senior engineer officer. 'The admiral's loo hasn't any water and Princess Margaret's in there!' I said. 'Tough,' he replied. 'There's always been a problem with those pipes. Nothing I can do!' Then sensing his promotion prospects could be rapidly disappearing unless he took matters into his own hands, he rushed from the wardroom to the auxiliary pumproom and opened every valve to increase the pressure in the ship's waste-disposal system.

I returned to the admiral's quarters to be met with the inevitable results of his efforts. The toilet had flushed successfully but, as so often happens on board ship, the sudden increase in pressure had resulted in a major eruption of water which drenched the admiral's wife as she attempted to depress the flush handle that had previously thwarted the royal visitor. Having suffered a downpour from above earlier the same evening, a similar effect was now being repeated from below. Perhaps dispirited by this turn of events, HRH decided it was time to leave and the upright grand piano remained unplayed.

POMP AND CIRCUMSTANCE

Before Princess Margaret's departure, the captain handed her a pen and invited her to sign the visitors' book. She leaned over to write her name. The pen made no imprint on the paper and HRH handed it back saying, 'First the ship with no water! Now the pen with no ink!' The captain cleared his throat in embarrassment, mumbled apologies and shook the pen vigorously before handing it back. HRH tried again. The pen still refused to write and again she handed it back, this time without a word. 'Has anyone here got a pen?' hissed the captain plaintively, trying to retrieve the situation. 'I've got a biro!' I replied, 'But the top's a bit chewed!' He snatched it from me and with a tooth-scarred, plastic ballpoint she at last managed her signature.

The tropical rain had returned as HRH walked down the gangway to leave the ship. It was now after midnight and whilst the royal party had been in the ship none of the crew, for security reasons, had been allowed to return on board. Nearly one hundred sailors had gathered in a harbour-side bar.

The effects of the strong local rum and Red Stripe beer were very obvious and the appearance of Princess Margaret on the gangway was greeted with loud cheers. Sheltering under a huge umbrella she smiled and waved. 'We love Princess Margaret! We love Tottenham too!' sang the sailors in football chanting tradition, together with clapping, stamping and a deafening 'You'll Never Walk Alone!' Stopping every few yards Princess Margaret, visibly moved, continued to acknowledge the sailors until she reached her official car.

It was a spontaneous, if incongruous farewell. Not only to Her Majesty's representative, but also to another small piece of the British Empire.

8

SHIPS' MATES

No one can be certain of the exact date when animals were first kept on board ships. There is plenty of evidence, however, that from the very earliest times sailing ships kept livestock on board, such as goats, pigs and chickens, to provide a ready source of fresh meat during long ocean voyages. It is also known that the crew sometimes become so fond of an animal that it would be kept as a pet instead of ending up on the dinner table.

In the same way that ships returning from tropical countries would bring back exotic birds and animals for zoos and menageries in Europe, the English King Henry I established his Royal Menagerie in 1125, so too some of these animals, especially monkeys and parrots who are naturally human-friendly, would be retained on board as ships' pets. Parrots, with their remarkable powers of mimicking the human voice, were favourites with seafarers and are, in the popular imagination, inextricably linked with pirates, thanks to Long

John Silver's parrot Captain Flint in Robert Louis Stevenson's *Treasure Island*.

Many cats and dogs, normally regarded as domestic pets, have spent their lives on board ship where they also served a practical purpose. Early woodblock illustrations show that buccaneers kept dogs on board and their name itself derives from the French *boucanier*, which referred to a person on the islands of Hispaniola and Tortuga in the Caribbean who used dogs for hunting wild oxen and boars.

With cats it was different. From the time of the ancient Egyptians, who took them on board their Nile river boats to catch birds in the thickets along the riverbanks, cats with their remarkable feline ability to adapt to new surroundings, have provided a ready means of keeping a ship's stores free from rodents. As official rat-catcher, a cat often became the ship's mascot.

Nevertheless, since 1975 all animals have been banned from Royal Naval ships on Health & Safety grounds, which, together with increased European legislation to prevent the spread of rabies and concerns over security, has seen the demise of ships' pets. In other countries, where the enforcement of such regulations is less rigorous, animals are still found on board naval ships, and scores of masters of merchant ships will rarely leave harbour without their cherished pet.

Stories of ship's pets and mascots in the past

provide a glimpse of their usefulness, sociability and bravery. When it comes to the latter, few can match Oscar the cat. Originally a survivor of the German battleship *Bismarck* when it was sunk in 1941, Oscar was picked up by the destroyer HMS *Cossack*, but when that ship was torpedoed a few months later, he again survived. This time he was taken on board HMS *Ark Royal* but shortly afterwards that ship was also sunk and Oscar once more was saved. Renamed 'Unsinkable Sam' he was put ashore to become official mouse-catcher to the Governor of Gibraltar and finished his days in a sailors' home in Belfast where he died in 1955.

Equally brave was Simon, the black-and-white tabby cat on board HMS *Amethyst* when the frigate was shelled by Chinese Communists on the River Yangtze in 1949. With twenty-five of the crew killed, and Simon singed and wounded by shrapnel, he continued with his rat-catching duties which were vitally important in protecting the ship's dwindling food supplies from rat-infestation. Simon died in quarantine after the ship returned to the UK and is buried in the PDSA cemetery in Ilford beneath a specially designed monument with the words 'His behaviour was of the highest order'. He was also posthumously awarded the Dickin Medal, often referred to as the 'Animal's VC'.

So highly regarded were ship's cats in the RN that many were given their own hammock complete with mattress, blanket and pillow. On Sundays an 'HMS' cap ribbon would be tied around their necks. In World War II the cruiser HMS *Hermione*'s cat, Convoy, so-called because of the number of times he had accompanied the ship on convoy duties, was listed as an 'Able-Bodied Cat' on the ship's books. The ship's cat on board the steam gunboat HM SGB–7, like the ship, had no name. He was known simply as 'TBC' – 'That Bloody Cat'!

A ship's cat which achieved lasting fame, and known affectionately as Mrs Chippy, sailed to Antarctica with Sir Ernest Shackleton's ill-fated expedition of 1914–15. The cat belonged to the Scottish-born carpenter Harry 'Chippy' McNeish whose carpentry skills ensured that a ship's lifeboat from the *Endurance*, after Shackleton's ship had been crushed in the ice, withstood the battering of some of the roughest seas in the world during its legendary 800 mile journey to South Georgia. In 2004 a life-size bronze statue of Mrs Chippy was erected over McNeish's grave in New Zealand.

The battleship HMS *Hood*, sunk in 1941 with the tragic loss of 1,415 lives, was well known for the variety of ship's pets acquired during a career spanning twenty-one years. These included a goat, an opossum, a squirrel, beavers and, most famous of all, Joey, a wallaby. Presented to the ship by the people of Australia during the ship's Empire cruise in 1924 he would box with crew members, perform tricks and, appropriately enough, had a liking for pouch tobacco! The ship's two cats, Fishcakes and Ginger, are believed to have perished with the ship.

In earlier times the battleship HMS *Ajax* was very proud of its adopted mascot, a black Russian bear appropriately named Trotsky, which had been acquired when the ship was serving in the Black Sea. In Malta in the 1920s Trotsky would sometimes go for a swim in the harbour but caused great consternation in the fleet if he returned to the wrong ship. When this happened a signal would be sent to HMS *Ajax* – 'Come and pick up your bear!'

Pets especially popular with captains of battleships were bulldogs. They were thought to epitomise the steadfast British 'John Bull' attitude of the 'Fear God, Dread Nought' Royal Navy of the early twentieth century. Other ship's pets of that era included a pig, Trotters, who evidently lived a life of pampered luxury on board the battle-cruiser HMS *Glasgow*, and a gazelle, Bill, mascot of the cruiser HMS *Highflyer* when it was serving on the Cape station.

When parrots and cockatoos were kept on board their perch had to be correctly aligned so they were not affected by the motion of the ship. A parrot smuggled on board the converted Ro-Ro ferry *MV Elk*, which sailed with the Task Force to the South Atlantic in 1982, achieved dubious notoriety after a doctor from the P&O

liner *Canberra* had to be called to administer emergency first aid when it broke a wing flying around its owner's cabin. Nearly a century earlier the schooner *Arbitrator*, fishing off the coast of Massachusetts, experienced a freak storm with hail the size of cobblestones, one of which killed the skipper's parrot which reputedly spoke three languages and had weathered the storms of twenty years at sea. The captain was said to be inconsolable.

In the early 1960s the tank landing ship HMS *Messina*, part of the Amphibious Warfare Squadron in Bahrain, had a pet monkey, Sippers, named after its habit of sipping the crew's midday rum ration. In the afternoons it would stretch out on the upper deck but after almost two years on board, Sippers disappeared one night at sea, believed to have fallen overboard having finally imbibed one tot too many!

Whilst recognising that ship's pets have served a wide variety of useful purposes, there seems little doubt that they also provide companionship, amusement and the enjoyment of looking after a dumb animal, thus allowing the seafarer a rare opportunity at sea of expressing feelings of love and affection.

Over a century ago the *New York Times* featured an article entitled 'Pets in the Fo'castle'. This aptly summed up a sailor's feelings about ships' pets. 'It affords him deep pleasure to hold in his loving though rough embrace the innocent creature who either by a cheerful wag of the tail, or a responsive purr, assures him that his attentions are appreciated.' Words as true today as when first written.

9

COLD WAR

During the long years of the Cold War it was standard practice for many naval officers serving ashore to hold what was known as a 'dormant appointment'. This would be in addition to their normal appointment but would only be activated if a certain state of readiness was announced and an attack on the United Kingdom, probably by the Soviet Union, was imminent. Details of such appointments were classified as 'Secret'.

Nevertheless, because of the difficulty in assessing the 'threat', and keeping up to date with technological advances in warfare, many such appointments often belonged to the 'Biggles to the Rescue' era, rather than having a pivotal role in President Reagan's fledgling 'Star Wars' programme.

As a young officer I was serving at the Royal Navy's fishery-protection base at South Queensferry on the shores of the River Forth in Scotland. One of this base's responsibilities, should hostilities commence, or the highest security state come into force, was the protection of a Royal Naval Armament Depot some sixty miles away in Ayrshire. As soon as the coded message confirming mobilisation had been received, my 'dormant appointment' would immediately come into force. This required me to become the officer in charge of a group of sailors tasked with the security of this depot and for putting it onto a war footing. We would be based there and expected to defend it to the last man.

Armament, ammunition and stores depots, as well as oil fuel storage tanks, were considered to be prime targets in the first stages of any global attack. However, as they were staffed entirely by Civil Service officers, clerks and storekeepers of the RN Supply and Transport Service – an arrangement dating back to Samuel Pepys who insisted that civilians rather than naval personnel should carry out these tasks in order to avoid the widespread corruption which riddled the eighteenth-century Navy – and with security provided by locally recruited Ministry of Defence police, they were something akin to slumbering giants when it came to maintaining the safety of the nation. The prosaic nature of their business dictated a regular nine-to-five routine and nearly thirty years of peace had rendered them extremely remote from any realities of the Cold War.

By tradition, all military and naval operations

are known by a code name. The code name given to the protection of the naval armament depot for which I would have responsibility was 'Operation Snapdragon'.

The orders for this operation were classified 'Secret' and kept locked in a safe at the naval base. A copy was also held at the depot. Security of documents was high priority as there was a danger of them being seen by spies or stolen by foreign agents. At the same time there was a requirement to activate dormant appointments from time to time to validate their relevance to the current security situation and to ensure that everyone involved knew exactly what to do. But to avoid any confusion between a real declaration of war and a rehearsal the code name would, in the latter case, always be prefaced by the word 'Exercise'.

On the first occasion it was decided to activate my own dormant appointment and carry out a routine check of the classified orders, a date was set in advance. Whilst the appropriate senior officers and myself knew this date it was not considered necessary for anyone else to know, including the armament depot, as this could compromise security. It was felt that the less people who knew that such an exercise was taking place the more realistic it would be. Such was the nature of the Cold War. Nevertheless, I was assured that those in key positions at the depot knew what 'Operation Snapdragon' signified – whether prefaced by 'Exercise' or not – and that it was a well-tried-and-tested operation.

The designated day in February dawned bleak and cold with rain blowing horizontally off the River Forth. Before climbing on board the blue RN bus, with surly civilian driver, I inspected my platoon of thirty-five sailors. They were dressed in camouflage fatigues and dark-blue berets and armed with the standard-issue automatic weapon – an SLR – although there was no ammunition. This was considered too dangerous for an exercise and, it was reasoned, there would be thousands of tons of it where we were going anyway. I was similarly attired but had a .38 revolver – also without ammunition – in a holster at my waist and a whistle on a white lanyard round my neck. 'All ready for the off, Sir!' reported my chief petty officer. 'Exercise Operation Snapdragon' had commenced.

The safe containing the classified orders was in the guardhouse at the entrance to the base. With the bus waiting outside, exhaust fumes vaporising into clouds of white smoke, and the glum, wan faces of my platoon staring through the rapidly misting-up windows, I opened the safe and withdrew a crimson folder marked 'Secret'. The instructions for 'Operation Snapdragon' were explicit. The telephone number of the depot was to be dialled. On receiving an answer I was to say only three words: 'Exercise Operation Snapdragon'. The person answering (the depot's switchboard operator) would simply repeat the words 'Exercise Operation Snapdragon'. I would then say 'ETA one hour forty-five minutes'. The operator would reply 'Roger'. The orders were unequivocal. No other words, greetings or conversation were to take place. If they did, the orders stressed, the whole exercise and its purpose would be jeopardised.

I dialled the number shown. After a long series of ringing tones a gruff Scottish voice answered with the name of the armament depot. 'Exercise Operation Snapdragon,' I said firmly into the mouthpiece. There was no reply. Just silence. I waited. The clock on the guardhouse wall ticked away the seconds. I decided I would have to try again. 'Exercise Operation Snapdragon,' I repeated, a little louder this time. 'I think you must have the wrong number,' said the now-irritated voice. 'This is the armament depot.' Things were not going at all according to plan. Had I said something incorrectly? Was this all part of a scheme to test my credentials? In desperation I repeated it a third time. 'Exercise Operation Snapdragon,' I shouted down the phone. 'Aye,' said the voice, 'I heard what youse said the first time but this is the armament depot and I think you've got the wrong number. Sorry. Goodbye.' The phone went dead.

The engine of the coach outside continued to emit clouds of smoke polluting the morning air. What was I to do? I was following the orders for a secret-coded operation and the only response I could get was someone saying that I had the wrong number! There was only one thing for it, I told myself, and that was to try again. If I compromised security then I would have to accept the consequences and probably face court martial.

Once again I dialled the number and again the same voice answered. I took a deep breath. 'This is the naval base HMS *Lochinvar* here,' I said slowly, 'and I am required to say to you the words "Exercise Operation Snapdragon".' There was a long moment of silence. 'Och aye,' the voice grumbled, 'I'll put you through to the police at the gate.' It was not exactly in accordance with the secret instructions but at least I was getting somewhere. Another heavily Scots-accented voice answered, 'Police, main gate,' and again I repeated what I had said to the exchange operator. Another long pause followed whilst, I assumed, the police officer was searching his memory for the correct response. 'Did ye say Exercise Operation Snapdragon, sir?' 'Yes,' I growled in frustration. 'Aye, I've heard aboot that. Just a minute and I'll take a look at the orders.'

So much, I thought, for classified material, secret code names and Russian spies. It was more like reporting the theft of a stolen bicycle. The policeman eventually returned to the telephone. 'Now I've had a look and did I hear you say you were from the naval base at South Queensferry, sir?' Any further pretence at security or worries I had about obeying the rules had now gone. 'Yes, that's right,' I replied, 'and we're coming over to your depot to carry out "Exercise Operation Snapdragon".' 'Aye,' he said, 'that's what it says here. What time do ye think you'll be arriving?' I told him that we would be there in one hour and forty-five minutes. At least that was in the orders. 'Look forward to seeing you then, sir!' he replied. That certainly was not. I wearily closed the folder, locked the safe and boarded the bus where everyone was waiting impatiently. 'Let's go, driver!' I instructed. 'Aye,' he muttered, 'an' aboot time too...!'

Our drive across the Scottish Lowlands was uninspiring. The sailors were complaining about the early start and the weather; the driver about the traffic and how he should never have been rostered for this job. But in spite of the inauspicious start to 'Exercise Operation Snapdragon' it was now time to move on to the next phase. This required me to telephone the armament depot when we were about five miles away in order to inform them of the precise time of our arrival and that they should have the gates open in readiness. We were, after all, a group of armed men undertaking an important operational exercise and no time was to be lost.

After an hour's driving I asked our driver to keep his eyes open for a telephone box so that I could make the necessary call. My platoon had no wireless equipment and this was long before mobile phones, so the only method of land communication was to use a public telephone box. The solidly built red boxes of that era were, however, notorious not only for their scarcity but also for their cumbersome equipment which required the caller to 'Press Button A' – a chunky chrome lever – before being connected. Eventually, as we approached a small village, the driver pointed out to me a red telephone box he could see down a deserted side road. This looked ideally situated so I ordered him to stop whilst I walked fifty or so yards in the drizzling rain to make my call.

As I approached the box it became apparent that it was already occupied by an elderly lady. Although I was certain she had noticed the movement of my approach, she deliberately turned her back to me and busied herself with her call. Once again this sort of delay, whilst not unexpected in public telephone boxes, could not have been anticipated when the orders for 'Operation Snapdragon' were originally written. I hoped her call would not last long. It was a forlorn hope.

After about three minutes I walked around the box to ensure that she was definitely aware that I was waiting to use the telephone. As I moved around the outside of the box so she too moved around the inside, so that I was always confronted by her back and her head bowed over the receiver. Another five minutes passed. I continued my deliberate and heavy booted circling of the box whilst the lady continued her shuffling, always presenting me with her broad back. This seemed as positive an indication as possible that she had no intention of cutting short her call and vacating the box so that I could use the telephone. With a bus full of impatient sailors at the end of the road, and the time stretching beyond our estimated arrival at the armament depot, how long, I wondered, could this charade continue?

Somehow I had to get the lady to finish her call. I rapped on the side of the box with a coin. At the sudden noise she turned and glared angrily as I mouthed the words, 'Can I use, please?' indicating the receiver she was holding whilst at the same time pointing to the coach waiting at the end of the road. It was to no avail. She shrugged her shoulders, turned her back and resumed her conversation.

Yet more frustrating minutes passed and with still no end to her call in sight I felt there was only one solution if 'Exercise Operation Snapdragon' was ever going to be completed that day. Again I tapped on the glass and as she turned around I snapped open the top of my holster and fingered the butt of my revolver. The message was plain. Confronted by a naval officer in battledress about to use his gun to take possession of a public telephone box in the middle of rural Scotland her resistance crumbled. She fumbled the phone back into its rest, found her handbag, pushed open the door and hurried past me without a backward glance. I could hear the ironic cheers of the sailors from the bus as at last I squeezed myself into the box.

I dialled the number and pressed Button A when the operator at the armament depot answered. 'Exercise Operation Snapdragon,' I said, 'We'll be with you in about ten minutes.' 'Aye,' he replied. 'What held ye up? We've been expecting you for a wee while noo!' Secure speech procedures were clearly redundant. I boarded the bus to a polite round of applause.

As expected, the gates of the armament depot were wide open when we arrived. I guess they probably had been for about the past hour. I deployed my security patrols to their pre-arranged areas and the petty officers dispersed to check that they were being properly carried out. The majority of the ammunition was stored in vast underground bunkers or in huge well-disguised hanger-like buildings. My command post was at the main gate where I spent a long and gloomy day drinking cups of tea, eating my packed lunch and trying to complete the crossword in *The Scotsman*. If this was to be my appointment when World War III started then I hoped it would, one way or another, all be over very quickly.

By dusk it was time to thank the civilian officers who had been so tolerant of an armed naval presence in their midst all day and prepare to return to the naval base. 'Probably see youse all again next year, sir,' said the police sergeant cheerily, as I shook hands before getting onto the bus. 'Yes,' I replied. 'Look forward to it!' Unless that is, I said to myself, the Russians get here first!

10

UP SPIRITS!

'Yo-ho-ho, and a bottle of rum!' sang the pirate Long John Silver in Robert Louis Stevenson's *Treasure Island*. As this memorable jingle never fails to remind, and as every advertising copywriter worth his salt knows, rum is inextricably linked with the sea, ships and the Navy. The Royal Navy in particular. Yet not a glass of it has been regularly issued to Her Majesty's sailors since 31 July 1970.

This was known as Black Tot Day and marked the last issue of rum in the Royal Navy. The *Portsmouth Evening News* recorded: 'sailors in ships and establishments in the area ... said farewell to the last issue of "Nelson's Blood" by conducting mock funerals and wearing black armbands...'

In the same way that rum has always been synonymous with everything nautical, the same might also have been said of rum's two most licentious companions, which together formed a notorious triumvirate and were, according to Winston Churchill, descriptive of the Royal Navy for nearly two centuries, namely 'Rum, Bum and Baccy'. They are, however, no longer a true reflection of life on the lower deck.

In the same way that the rum issue was abolished, so the others have been mortally wounded. 'Baccy' by the government's ban on smoking in public places, and 'bum' by the legalisation of such behaviour between consenting male adults in private, although not amongst servicemen. The salty and rumbustious days which spawned this derogatory description of the senior service are gone for good!

Rum as the special naval tipple, however, has a fascinating history. Originally it was the quality of beer on board ship, once referred to by a seventeenth-century sea captain as 'stinking', and the difficulties of obtaining and keeping fresh water, that led directly to the issue of rum. In spite of Samuel Pepys' improvements in administration and victualling there were no overseas bases and, with British expansion in the Americas and West Indies, it became commonplace for individual ships, when visiting the islands, to stock up on the cheap local brew.

On 14 February 1727, the captain of HMS *Greyhound* in Port Royal, Jamaica, complaining about the lethargy of his crew in helping to build a new jetty, wrote to the Admiralty: 'If anything can make life agreeable to them, it may be a double allowance of rum being joined to what extra pay maybe thought proper'. As his ship's company were already receiving half a pint of rum per man per day as an alternative to their allowance of beer, which was eight pints per man per day, the Captain's recommendation implied that his men should have a pint of rum every day to make them work harder!

Against this background, and with more ships visiting the West Indies, the first official approval to issue rum on a daily basis was given in 1731. By the end of that decade, although still largely confined to ships deployed to the Caribbean, the practice of daily rum issue had become widespread. The rum was drunk undiluted and this inevitably led to many accidents at sea, as well as drunkenness on board in harbour. The press-ganged crews were not allowed shore leave but this did not stop them smuggling quantities of rum on board in coconuts, which they cleverly drained of their milk. This was known as 'sucking the monkey' and, together with the custom of permitting local women to share a sailor's hammock, resulted in further indiscipline and calls for stringent action.

Vice Admiral Edward Vernon, as Commander-in-Chief of the West Indies Station, was appalled at the drunkenness of his fleet. In 1740 he ordered:

Whereas the pernicious custom of the seaman drinking their allowance of rum in drams, and often at once, is attended by many fatal effects to their morals as well as their health, the daily issue of half a pint is to be diluted with a quart of water to be mixed in one scuttle-butt ... in the presence of the Lieutenant of the Watch.

This mixture immediately become known as 'grog' due to the Admiral's nickname 'Old Grog', so called because he wore a boat cloak made of grogram ('grosgrain'), a coarse waterproof mixture of mohair and silk. The issue was permitted twice per day, at noon and sunset. As a result, drunkenness become less prevalent and the rate of sickness, which hitherto had such a debilitating effect upon the crews of ships serving in tropical waters, was reduced.

In the following years grog-drinking spread, as more ships from the West Indies arrived back in England with full casks of rum in their holds. It also became necessary to have a separate stowage where the neat rum could be safely stored. This compartment, which became known as the 'Spirit Room', was built into every warship constructed for the next two hundred years.

Nevertheless, it took another forty years for the Admiralty to reluctantly accept that rum was in the Navy to stay. It was not until 1784 that James Man, a merchant dealing in imported goods from the West Indies, was appointed as official rum-broker. The rum was shipped direct to bonded warehouses where it was bought by the Navy's victualling department and stored at the new yards being built at Gosport and Devonport. The raw rum was specified as 40 per cent over proof and the firm, which became known as ED & F Man, continued to supply rum to the Royal Navy until the final issue.

Throughout Nelson's time in command in the Caribbean, as well as during his later triumphs in the Napoleonic War, grog as originally constituted continued to be issued twice daily. However, in 1824 on the recommendation of Admiral Lord Keith, still concerned at the habitual drunkenness in the fleet, the issue was reduced further – to one gill of rum, to which was added two equal parts of water, issued once per day 'to every victualled member of the Ship's Company who were over the age of 20 years and who were not temperant'.

Although the Board of Admiralty might well have felt that this reform would reduce drunkenness, it is worth recalling that a gill was then equal to a quarter of a pint. So the Navy rum issue, equivalent in strength to four double whiskies today, and in spite of being diluted with water to form grog, was still a lethal drink irrespective of the time of day when it was consumed. It was this ration, although later reduced in 1850 to half a gill (equal to one gill or an eighth of a pint in modern terms), that continued to be issued until 1970.

Then senior service officers and a campaigning parliamentary lobby, recognising the increased technological complexity of ships and naval warfare, recommended that the issue of grog to sailors, and neat spirit to chief petty officers and petty officers in the traditional strength and quantity, should be discontinued.

It was recognised, however, that abolition would be universally unpopular. So the Navy Minister, Dr David Owen, Labour MP for Devonport, reluctant to be involved in what he perceived as a vote-losing act with serving sailors and thousands of ex-matelots, many of them in his constituency, proposed instead that a reasonable daily beer ration should be provided to junior ratings, and that chief and petty officers should be permitted similar drinking privileges, both beer and a range of duty-free spirits, to those that officers had always enjoyed. He also argued that the equivalent of three pence per day, which was the sum paid to those sailors who did not 'draw a tot' and who were designated by a 'T' for Temperance, should be paid by the government for every rating serving at the time.

This, together with £2.7 million provided by the Treasury, to compensate for the purchase of rum from traditional sources, was used to set up a fund known as the Royal Naval Sailor's Fund. Immediately this became known as 'The Tot Fund' and exists to the present day helping to finance a range of sporting and welfare amenities for sailors not provided by the Ministry of Defence.

UP SPIRITS!

The unenviable task of informing the Royal Navy that the issue of rum, after nearly 230 years, was finished fell to the First Sea Lord, Admiral of the Fleet Sir Michael Le Fanu. Nicknaming himself, both because of his sandy hair and this historic act of temperance, 'Dry Ginger', he signalled to the fleet:

Most farewell messages try to tear-jerk the tear from the eye,
But I say to you lot, Very sad about tot,
And thank you, good luck and goodbye.

The Board of Admiralty introduced the compensatory measures already approved and then, in 1979, in a remarkable act of foresight and entrepreneurial flair, sanctioned the sale of the special blending formula which for so long had been a closely guarded secret, together with the distillery in Tortola in the British Virgin Islands which had been supplying rum since the earliest days, to an American millionaire businessman, Charles Tobias.

The rum is distilled in a process not unlike that used for the best single malt whiskies. By using the original pot stills the rum has a unique flavour which has been absorbed in the wood from which they were first constructed. It is alleged that Nelson, before capturing Tortola and proclaiming it a Crown Colony, had trained his guns on the capital, Road Town, and threatened to blow the inhabitants into the Caribbean, only to grant a reprieve when the island offered, in exchange for clemency, an unlimited supply of rum to the Royal Navy in perpetuity.

Mr Tobias, in partnership first of all with the long-established ED & F Man, began marketing the rum worldwide as Pusser's Rum using the White Ensign as his company's logo. 'Pusser', a corruption of the word *purser*, the officer aboard ship responsible for providing food and stores, was also naval jargon for anything that was official. Hence rum was 'pusser' being Admiralty-approved and issued from the purser's department. Mr Tobias has also been a generous benefactor from the profits of his sales and makes a royalty donation to the 'Tot Fund' for every bottle of Pusser's Rum sold.

Despite the elaborate funeral rites enacted a generation ago there will be only a handful of sailors today who will have experienced rum's sacrosanct traditions. For the issue of rum, and grog, like so many naval customs had a time-honoured routine as well as its own special language. Sailors were expected to remove their headgear in respect to the monarch when receiving their rum ration issued from the tub on which was emblazoned in large brass letters 'The Queen God Bless Her'. The daily issue of grog was supervised, as tradition demanded, by the officer of the day and a petty officer, assisted by the 'tanky' – usually a long-serving sailor whose name derived from the days when the sailing master's assistant looked after the freshwater tanks – and the 'Jack Dusty' – another sailor so called after his original storekeeping duties in the dusty breadroom and whose job it was to account for the rum and take care of the assortment of copper measures and lipped jugs.

The rum was collected by sailors in receptacles known as 'fannies'. Reputedly called after Fanny Adams, a lady of dubious repute, whose remains, after her murder in the Deptford victualling yard in the late nineteenth century, were said to have been mixed with the preserved mutton which was then issued to the fleet in large round tins. It was also the sailors' ribald explanation of why members of the Women's Royal Naval Service (known as Wrens) did not receive an issue of rum, because if they did, 'They would have to hold out their fanny and say "Sir"!'

Neither did officers ever receive rum, except on the occasion of the order 'splice the mainbrace' when an extra tot was issued to every person serving on board or possibly the entire fleet. This could be in recognition of a special event – for instance a visit by the sovereign, a coronation, a fleet review, or before or after a battle. The expression derived from the days of sail when if the mainbrace parted in a storm (the braces were the lines used to trim the sails which, in the heaviest rigging, could be up to 20 inches in diameter) it had to be spliced together again, still in bad weather. This was a tough and skilled job so those who carried it out were rewarded with an extra tot of rum for their efforts.

Drinking a tot of rum also had its own vocabulary. 'Neaters' was the neat rum issued to senior ratings. 'Queen's', or alternatively 'plushers', was anything left over after the issue – and so called as belonging to the Queen – and traditionally passed around those present at the time. A 'wet' was just enough to wet your lips; 'sippers', a small, polite sip from a friend's issue; 'gulpers', a good swallow, probably in return for a favour granted or a duty carried out on a friend's behalf; and 'sandy bottoms', the invitation to drink whatever was left in shipmate's mug or glass. Rum was also a form of shipboard currency which had its own equivalent values. Three 'wets' equalled one 'sip'; three 'sips' equalled one 'gulp'; and three 'gulps' equalled one tot. Woe betide anyone who tried to abuse the system! A sailor who had a good nose for where he might find, or be given, an extra tot, or even a sip of rum, was known as a 'Rum Rat'.

Today selected off-licences stock Pusser's Rum and duty-free outlets around the world do a brisk trade (see the recipe for a delicious – and intoxicating – Pusser's Rum punch at the end of the chapter). But reaching for a bottle of the dark, mahogany-hued liquid from a shelf is a far cry from being on board one of Her Majesty's

UP SPIRITS!

ships and hearing, at precisely 11.50 a.m. each day, 'Up Spirits' trilled on the boatswain's call to announce that the daily rum issue was taking place. In the same way that old salts would mutter, 'Standfast the Holy Ghost!' on hearing these hallowed words, so all such phantoms and fantasies are now permanently laid to rest.

This nostalgia is epitomised in a poem written by a sailor in Portsmouth on the day rum issue in the Royal Navy finally came to an end:

At ten to twelve each forenoon
Since the Navy first began
Jack drank the health of Nelson
From Jutland to Japan

He's always done his duty
To country and the throne
And all he asks in fairness
Is leave his tot alone

You soothed my nerves
And warmed by limbs
And cheered my dismal heart
Procured my wants, obliged my whims
But now it's time to part

And so the time has come, old friend
To take the final sup
Our tears are shed, this is the end
Goodbye and Bottoms Up!

CALL THE HANDS

Recipe for Pusser's Rum Punch

Ingredients
2 tbsp sugar
zest and juice of 1 lemon
1/2 pint (300 ml) – 1 cup – Pusser's Rum
1/8 pint (75 ml) – 1/4 cup – brandy
1 pint (600 ml) – 2 cups – boiling water

Method
Use a very large saucepan with a tightly fitting lid.

Put the sugar and lemon zest into the saucepan with the rum and brandy. Warm the mixture over a medium heat until the sugar has melted, turn off the heat and set light to the mixture. Let it burn for 2 minutes, then cover the saucepan to extinguish the flame. Squeeze the juice from the lemon and add it to the mixture along with the boiling water. Stir well, cover and leave to stand for 5–10 minutes. Taste and add more sugar if deemed necessary before serving.

Traditional RN Toasts

Monday	'To our ships at sea'
Tuesday	'To our men'
Wednesday	'To ourselves – as no one is likely to concern themselves with our welfare'
Thursday	'To a bloody war and quick promotion'
Friday	'To a willing soul and sea room'
Saturday	'To sweethearts and wives ... may they never meet!'
Sunday	'To absent friends and those at sea'

But the standing toast that pleased the most was:

To the wind that blows,
The ship that goes,
And the lass that loved a sailor!

11

CHILLED OUT

One essential ingredient for drinks in hot climates is that they have either been kept in a refrigerator or they have plenty of ice in them. A drink without ice in the tropics, particularly a mixed one, is hardly a drink at all.

The admiral's buffet lunch party on the quarterdeck of the aircraft carrier anchored in Montego Bay, Jamaica, was an important occasion. The guests were diplomats and their wives who would arrive by helicopter from Kingston. The brass dolphins had been polished, the scuppers freshly painted and the decks scrubbed. The huge ship swung lazily at anchor in a translucent sea which lapped at the sandy beaches that form a natural break from the green hillsides surrounding this famous anchorage. A gentle offshore breeze tempered the fierceness of the noon sun but hardly disturbed the crisp white cloths spread over trestle tables. As a host officer I looked across to the shore where the rich and famous have their residences discreetly visible amidst lush tropical vegetation. The helicopter was due to arrive in five minutes and everything was ready. Except there was no ice.

For all the ship's modern technology there was no ice for the admiral or his guests. The chief steward had discovered this catastrophe when he went to the ice-making machine which had been working overtime and found there would be no new ice for a further three hours. It was also too late to try and get some from ashore. As ambassadors for Her Majesty's government part of our role was to provide official hospitality at a high level but to attempt to do this in the tropics without ice would not be acceptable.

A message then arrived that the helicopter had been delayed for forty-five minutes. It was just the news we needed. If sufficient ice was available from ashore there might be enough time to get there in a fast boat and return for the delayed lunch. Speed, time and distance were swiftly calculated and the Montego Bay Yacht Club, whose jetty could be seen across the bay, confirmed they had sufficient ice for our needs. The challenge was on.

The fastest sea boat was the admiral's launch, but it would have to go at full throttle if it was to reach the yacht club and return. A driver was summoned and the admiral's personal steward, who had been anticipating serving drinks from

CHILLED OUT

a silver tray, was entrusted with the task of returning with the ice. Forty minutes remained. It was 'Mission Just Possible'!

On Leading Steward Jimmy Green the success of the admiral's lunch party now depended. He scrambled down to the waiting launch and with a roar and sharp turn it sped away from the ship. We could only stand and watch as the boat, bouncing across the waves with Green hanging on grimly, cut a white swathe of foam through the azure water. The admiral, realising that the success of his lunch now rested in the hands of his steward, watched through a telescope and paced impatiently. 'Can't he go any faster?' he growled. 'At this rate we'll only be having iced coffee!' The further away into the midday haze the boat went so it seemed the plan was doomed to failure.

A message then came that the helicopter carrying the guests was expected in thirty-five minutes. The admiral stopped pacing and focused his telescope. 'I think he's nearly at the jetty! Yes, he must be climbing up! Quickly, man! He's running along it. Faster, faster! Go into the clubhouse!' he urged. An agonising wait followed as the steward disappeared from site. Further exhortations were fruitless.

A message from the ship's bridge reported 'ETA admiral's helo seventeen minutes, sir.' 'Oh, come on, Green,' urged the waiting officers but there was still no sign of the steward. Or the ice. An officer with binoculars then shouted, 'It looks like he's got it!' and relayed that Green could be seen staggering down the jetty carrying a large bag. The launch was moored out of sight so it was impossible to see precisely what was happening. All we knew was that with every minute that passed the helicopter would be getting closer.

The tense atmosphere was suddenly broken by another excited shout. The launch could be seen rounding the end of the jetty and was heading back towards the ship. 'Go for it, Green!' everyone urged, leaning on the guardrails as if in the grandstand at Epsom! 'Come on! You can do it!' The tiny dark-blue boat with its bow wave was now clearly visible and news that the helicopter was also visible only increased the excitement. Who would arrive first? Guests or ice? We watched as the boat continued its rapid progress and heard the helicopter as it started to circle the ship.

'Another two hundred yards and he'll be here!' muttered the admiral, realising that diplomatic embarrassment might, after all, be avoided. The noise of the helicopter drowned our voices and the downdraught flattened the sea. We heard the thump as it landed on the flight deck. There would still be a few minutes before the guests were escorted safely from the aircraft. The admiral's launch was now almost alongside and Green, soaked with seaspray, could be seen clutching a large plastic bag of ice. 'Well done! You've made it!' we shouted. The boat's engine stopped, the chief steward threw down a rope and we hauled up the precious cargo. The contents were quickly emptied into waiting ice buckets and a sense of quiet efficiency returned.

The British High Commissioner's wife stepped onto the quarterdeck followed by the other guests. 'Welcome aboard!' said the admiral, calm and self-assured, shaking her hand, 'I'm sure you'd love a drink after your journey!' 'Oh, yes!' she enthused, 'And please make sure there's plenty of ice!' 'Of course, madam,' said the chief steward with a smile, 'No problem at all.'

12

PAWS FOR THOUGHT

It was not intended to be a holiday for my family. But when my Royal Navy appointer said, 'We've pencilled you in for Hong Kong for three years,' that was what, at first, it seemed. I could hardly believe my good fortune. Bubbling with excitement, I telephoned home. 'At least we'll be able to have some time abroad with the children,' enthused my wife. 'They'll be over the moon when we tell them.' 'I sincerely hope so,' I replied. 'Let's tell the three of them together.'

'Well,' I announced a little later to my assembled offspring, a broad smile on my face, 'I've got some really good news. I've been posted to Hong Kong and we're all going to live there!' My daughter, then aged four, grinned happily. My sons, aged ten and eleven, from whom I was expecting whoops of excitement and imitation kung-fu kicks, sat glum and unsmiling. At last, after an eerie silence, the eldest gulped, 'But will we be able to take the pets?' The pets were three gerbils and a mouse. 'Of course not,' I laughed. 'Just give them to your friends.' 'If we can't take the pets then we shan't go!' he said grimly. Things were not going at all as planned.

Over the next weeks I cajoled, I offered bribes, but there was no changing the childrens' minds. No pets – no go. There was only one alternative – take the animals as well. As soon as this was promised, the gloom lifted. Excited planning started in earnest. The airline was helpful. To them carrying a cargo of livestock around the world was an everyday event. Yes, our animals were very small and whilst they were more used to transporting larger species, they said ours would be a 'drop in the ocean'. With a hasty apology for this inappropriate metaphor, they sent the necessary documentation.

International regulations for the transport of animals and birds by air, from which gerbils and mice are not excluded, are voluminous. Everything was detailed. The precise dimensions of the box. The thickness of wood. Each box to be lined with exact-sized wire mesh. Unless the containers conformed, our pets would not be going anywhere. We decided they would have to share accommodation, and at a cost of £80 for two bespoke boxes, they would definitely be travelling first class.

Animals, like humans going abroad, also require vaccination. 'But it will set you back £10 per jab,' said our vet, 'so I would just tell your children that the wee things passed away under anaesthetic.' Heedless of his advice, the inoculations went ahead and I paid up. The Department of Agriculture and Fisheries in Hong Kong also had to be informed, with reasons given for importing live animals, together with their age, medical history and 'availability for inspection while resident'. The paperwork for each tiny animal mounted. My purpose in going to Hong Kong became forgotten in making the arrangements for three gerbils and a mouse.

A large hangar at Gatwick's International Cargo Terminal was our pets' own executive check-in. A white-coated handler examined the documents and peered into the livestock-labelled boxes: 'These air holes don't look big enough, but I'll get the vet to check.' I hoped he was wrong but the vet announced brusquely that the apertures were insufficient for two animals in each box and must be enlarged before travel. This is similar to finding you've arrived with excess baggage and have no credit cards, cheque or cash with which to pay. In this case I had no tools with which to make the holes larger, insufficient wire mesh to cover them and our own check-in deadline to meet. Sincerely wishing, not for the first time, that I had never embarked on this whole zoo trip, the vet finally agreed to try and enlarge the holes himself, although he could not guarantee the security of the animals. I decided that if 'a drop in the ocean' did occur, I would tell the children it was the fortunes of war.

CALL THE HANDS

Our arrival in Hong Kong, at the end of a high-humidity day and after a seventeen-hour flight, did not inspire optimism as I set off to find the equivalent of Baggage Reclaim (Small Animals). If it doesn't come to Hong Kong by sea, it comes by air. Mountains of boxes, the whirl of fork-lift trucks, lines of uniformed customs officers, and sweating coolies confronted me. Clutching my forms, I explained to an impatient immigration officer that I had come to collect two boxes containing three gerbils and a mouse.

'Wha gebbil?' he grunted. 'Wha mouse?' It was clear from the piled containers that fresh food arrives everyday from all over the world. Knowing the Chinese appetite for live animal delicacies, it seemed that I was suspected of trying to illegally import some form of exotic hors d'oeuvre. I explained they were pets. 'Wha pet?' he insisted. 'For my children,' I replied.

At that moment a customs officer arrived with our two expensive cages still intact, despite Gatwick's crude joinery. I peered inside and sharp movements and bright eyes assured me all was well. 'Wha gerbil?' the official repeated. 'A form of rat,' I replied. 'A lat? Why you bling lat Hong Kong? I want look see,' he said.

The carefully constructed boxes were prized open. The largest gerbil, sensing freedom, leapt into the air. The Chinese official, visibly shaken, leapt backwards. 'OK! OK! You go! You take lat!'

The lid to the box was quickly secured, my

forms stamped and unceremoniously I was pushed into the oriental night. Next day I wrote to my sons at school in England, where they awaited their flight to Hong Kong: 'Arrived safely. Wish you were here. Signed Herbie, Phillipa, Thumper and Hans (mouse).' My Far East posting, and the holiday for three gerbils and a mouse, had begun.

13

OVER THE TOP

Most of us are always keen to get it right when we start on something new. This was certainly the case when, as a sixteen-year-old boy straight from grammar school, I joined the Royal Navy as a rating and arrived at Victoria Barracks in Portsmouth.

The first two days passed in a blur of attending lectures, being issued with our kit, and receiving a multitude of instructions which included how to march, and when to salute. Everything was completely alien but, as we were frequently reminded, 'You're in the Navy now,' and there would be dire consequences if we did not at all times obey orders. Many of these, often rife with apparent contradictions, were difficult to comprehend.

Not least the regulations regarding the wearing of your uniform hat, known in naval terminology as 'headgear'. Your hat must be worn, we were told, at all times, whether ashore or afloat, except in our messes or when having a meal. This was coupled with orders about how and when to salute an officer, whom you always had to salute when meeting or passing except when in regular contact on board ship or on railway stations. To salute correctly, it was stressed, you also had to be wearing your hat so that you did not appear to be, as it was graphically described, 'like a penguin flapping its f*****g wings'! I found it all extremely confusing.

Eventually my determination to do things correctly was put to the test. On my third day I had to use the toilet, known in naval terminology as 'the heads'. In the naval barracks this was a long line of old-fashioned cubicles with ill-fitting doors and a large space both above and below flimsy wooden partitions. But as soon as I had locked the door behind me I realised that I did not know whether I should keep my hat on my head or remove it.

I could not recall any mention being made about what was the correct naval procedure to be followed in the circumstances in which I now found myself. My mind was so full of the times when your hat did, or did not, need to be worn, and fearful of committing a monumental breach of service etiquette so early in my new career, there seemed to be only one solution. Check on the sailor in the adjoining cubicle to see whether or not he was wearing his hat whilst using the heads. I knew the cubicle was in use as I could hear the occupant and see his shoes and rumpled trousers under the partition.

OVER THE TOP

Plucking up courage, and with my hat firmly on my head, I stood on the toilet seat and very quietly, with my hands resting on top of the partition, nervously peered over the top. Despite my precautions, the sailor using the toilet clearly sensed that something was amiss and looked up. Momentarily our eyes met. 'F**k off, you dirty bastard!' he growled, gesticulating furiously. Panic-stricken and shamefaced I jumped hurriedly down. But in the confusion caused by my attempt to check on my neighbour's headgear, I had totally forgotten to notice whether, in fact, he was wearing his hat!

Still faced with the dilemma of not knowing whether it was correct to remove one's headgear when using the heads, and despite the anger I had encountered, I decided there was no alternative but to take another look. In my innocence, I did not realise that my action might be construed as that of a man wanting to solicit another for sexual activity, which, in the grubby anonymity of the heads in a crowded naval barracks, was not unknown. Nevertheless, with such thoughts furthest from my mind, I again climbed onto the toilet seat and cautiously looked over the partition into the next cubicle. The other sailor, doubtless unsettled by his voyeuristic experience moments before, glanced upwards.

Determined this time to explain that my action was harmless, I blurted out in a trembling voice, 'I'm so sorry to bother you but I only wanted to see if you were wearing your hat!' Now even more enraged by this wholly unbelievable and bizarre explanation, he launched into another tirade shouting, 'Why don't you get your f*****g thrills elsewhere, you little pervert!' After which he stood up, flushed the toilet and left, banging the door behind him. I could still hear his angry oaths as he stormed out of the building. Hugely embarrassed, I finished my own use of the heads and departed, fervently hoping that I would never encounter the same sailor again.

A long time passed before I felt sufficiently recovered from my humiliation to recount this experience to a friend. Although astonished by my naivety, he was more intrigued to know whether, in the end, I had discovered if the sailor in the next cubicle was, or was not, wearing his hat. I must confess, however, that decades later I still do not know the answer...!

14

ENGLAND EXPECTS

Horatio Nelson, although neither a true 'Man of Kent' nor a 'Kentish Man', had a long and distinguished association with that county.

He was born at Burnham Thorpe in Norfolk on 29 September 1758, one of eight children of the Reverend Edmund Nelson whose father had also been a country clergyman. There was nothing therefore particularly remarkable about his parentage on his father's side. But his mother, Catherine, who died when he was nine years old, could trace descendancy from Sir Robert Walpole, Britain's first Prime Minister, and one of her brothers, Captain Maurice Suckling, was a successful naval officer.

At the age of twelve, and still at school in North Walsham, young Horatio heard that his Uncle Maurice had been appointed to command the *Raisonnable* fitting out for overseas service. Excited by this news he begged his father to write and ask if he could go with him. Captain Suckling agreed, writing back:

What has poor Horace done, who is so weak that he, above all the rest, should be sent to rough it out at sea? But let him come and the first time we go into action a cannon-ball may knock off his head and provide for him at once.

Undeterred by this reply, he went with his father in early 1771 by stagecoach to London. From there he took the Brompton stage to Chatham which stopped outside the main gate to the dockyard. This building with the coat of arms of George III above the entrance remains unchanged to this day. The naval career of Mr Midshipman Nelson, and his lifelong association with the county of Kent, had begun.

His introduction to the Navy, however, was inauspicious for no one knew where the *Raisonnable* was berthed. It was not until a kindly former naval officer took pity on the young man that he found his way to the ship. At that time ships which had just left the dockyard were moored in the River Medway opposite Upnor Castle. This required Nelson to walk through the dockyard to what was known as Princes Bridge and from there get a boat out to his ship.

In doing so, he would certainly have walked past the dock where his future flagship, the *Victory*, was being fitted out. This famous ship had been ordered by the Admiralty in the year of his birth and the keel laid down in Chatham a year later. It is not hard to imagine how thrilled the young midshipman must have been on seeing his very first warship. The same ship that thirty-four years later was, by coincidence, destined to be the scene of his greatest triumph and heroic death.

However, as the *Raisonnable* was subsequently not required for service overseas, Captain Suckling was given command of the *Triumph*, a guardship in the River Medway. It was from this ship that young Nelson piloted the ship's sailing cutter and learned to navigate the shoals and tides of the rivers Thames, Medway and Swale. The confidence he gained in such restricted waters was to stand him in good stead for the remainder of his career.

Chatham in the latter half of the eighteenth century was Britain's premier naval dockyard and most of the buildings of that period have survived to this day. Between 1700 and the end of the Napoleonic Wars, Chatham Dockyard built over a hundred ships for the Royal Navy. Repairs and maintenance of other ships provided work for nearly 1,500 men throughout this period. The *Victory* took six years to build at a cost of £63,176, equivalent to the cost of a modern aircraft carrier in today's money. Construction required the wood of 6,000 trees, mainly oak, plus elm, pine and fir, 27 miles of rope for the rigging and 4 acres of canvas for the sails.

Because of Chatham's distance from the open

sea it could sometimes take twelve weeks for large vessels to sail down the River Medway. This led to the establishment of a naval dockyard in Sheerness. It was also close to the important anchorage of The Nore, the name given to the waters off the north Kent coast across the mouth of the Thames to Essex.

On 9 April 1777 when Nelson had completed six years' sea service he received his commission as Second Lieutenant of the frigate *Lowestoffe*, which he joined at Sheerness. The ship did not sail immediately so he took the opportunity to visit London and have his portrait painted by John Francis Rigaud. This is now in the National Maritime Museum, Greenwich. But because the painting was not finished until 1780, it was altered to show him as a proud twenty-one-year-old captain in the West Indies, although his features remain those of the fresh-faced young man he was when the painting was started.

Nelson returned to Sheerness in 1787 as captain of the *Boreas* after his second cruise to the Caribbean. During this time he had married a widow, Frances Nisbet, on the island of Nevis. The future King William IV, then Captain William Henry, was at Nelson's side and gave away the bride. In Sheerness, Nelson's ship was used as the receiving ship for men recruited by the press gangs which were then operating in many Kentish towns. Shortly afterwards, hostilities with France came to an end and as there was no employment for Nelson he returned home to Norfolk for five years. There he lived the life of a country gentleman but all the while yearned to get back to sea.

It was not until war clouds were again gathering that Nelson returned to Kent. This time to take command of his first ship of the line, the *Agamemnon*, fitting out at Chatham. The circumstances were very different from his first visit. He was now an experienced captain, married and with a midshipman stepson, Josiah, who joined the ship with him. On 7 February 1793 he called on the Resident Commissioner of the Dockyard in the magnificent house which still exists. It is the oldest British naval building to survive intact. Captain Nelson in full dress uniform, cocked hat and sword then walked the few hundred yards to what is now known as the Assistant Queen's Harbour Master's Office on Thunderbolt Pier to be rowed out to his new command.

His ship did not go downriver until mid-March and, although he visited his wife on a number of occasions, he did not ask her to join him at Sheerness where the Three Tuns was acclaimed by naval officers, with a sort of perverted pride, as 'The Worst Inn in the World'. In a month at the port he never slept ashore and his cabin in the *Agamemnon*, in which he was to see continuous service in the Mediterranean for the next three years, was his home. It was during these years that he first met Emma Hamilton, wife of Sir William, the British ambassador in Naples.

It was also during this time the infamous mutinies took place on board ships anchored at The Nore. This was especially frightening for those in the dockyards at Chatham and Sheerness who feared the revolution which was sweeping France might spread to the entire British fleet. Richard Parker, the ringleader of the mutineers, was hanged on board the *Sandwich* anchored at the mouth of the Medway on 30 June 1797. Twenty-nine of his fellows suffered the same fate in the following weeks.

Nelson did not return to England until September 1797. By then he had lost the sight of his right eye at Calvi in Corsica and his right arm at Santa Cruz in Tenerife. Although hailed as a hero after his exploits at the Battle of Cape St Vincent and promoted to Rear Admiral, his victories at the Battle of the Nile and the Battle of Copenhagen were yet to come. When, in 1801, he returned home from these it was natural he would be first choice to repel the threat of invasion by Napoleon which once again was very real. Nelson was therefore appointed in charge of the naval forces and went on board his flagship the *Unite* at Sheerness. The country was on war alert, particularly in Kent where the citizens of Margate, Ramsgate, Dover and Folkestone were making plans for evacuation.

On 28 July 1801 Nelson issued orders to the

ships under his new command, some of which had appropriate names – *Defender, Conflict, Attack, Gallant* – and by the next day was ready to leave, by post-chaise, for Deal and Faversham. His arrival in Faversham attracted large cheering crowds and he inspected the reservists who looked 'with wild but affectionate amazement at him who was once more going to step forward in defence of his country'.

Deal was important to the Navy as it was the port for The Downs, the protected anchorage in the lee of the Goodwin Sands, where as many as 300 ships could lie safely offshore. There was also a walled dockyard which built small sailing vessels, carried out ship repairs and supplied stores, provisions and fresh water to the anchored ships. It covered a large area of the town with the main entrance adjacent to the Port Arms public house and the Time Ball Tower, which both still exist. In August 1801, with invasion likely from France just twenty-two miles away, Deal was a scene of great activity.

Nelson took the opportunity not only to command his ships from there but also to have a brief family holiday by the sea. Lady Nelson as well as Sir William and Lady Hamilton arrived in Deal to stay at the Three Kings (now The Royal Hotel) where Nelson booked rooms with a gallery overlooking the beach. A bathing machine was hired for the ladies. During this time they made excursions to Ramsgate, Dover

Castle and Walmer. This was an unusual *ménage à quatre*, as Nelson had also become the father of a daughter, Horatia, born to Emma Hamilton earlier the same year.

Using knowledge gleaned from local smugglers who brought back information as well as brandy and tobacco, Nelson planned to attack the enemy flotilla in Boulogne harbour with ships and flat-bottomed barges loaded with explosives. The expedition, however, was a failure, with 44 men killed and 128 wounded. Captain Edward Parker, one of Nelson's most promising young officers, was severely wounded and the admiral took lodgings for him at 73 Middle Street so he could recover. This narrow street of Georgian houses still exists, largely unchanged. However, the young man died and is buried in St George's churchyard. Nelson attended the funeral as chief mourner and was observed leaning on an oak tree weeping bitterly.

During the so called 'experimental peace' with France that followed it seems likely that Nelson visited Sheerness again and with Lady Hamilton stayed at Church House in nearby Queenborough. It is believed they worshipped together in Holy Trinity Church. He was then sent to command the Mediterranean fleet in the *Victory*, which between 1800 and 1803 had been completely refitted in Chatham Dockyard at a cost greater than building the ship there forty years earlier.

Nelson's final return to Kent was after the

Battle of Trafalgar on 21 October 1805 when his battle-scarred flagship *Victory*, under makeshift masts and sails, anchored off Deal on 19 December. This time the flags in the dockyard and the town were at half mast. Delayed by two days of gales, the ship eventually sailed round to The Nore where the surgeon Sir William Beatty performed an autopsy on the admiral's body, preserved in a cask of brandy after the battle, and extracted the fatal musket bullet.

Nelson was in his forty-eighth year. His body was transferred to a coffin which he had had made especially for himself from the wood of the main mast of *L'Orient*, a captured French ship. The county's adopted 'Man of Kent' had come home for the last time. The nation was in mourning.

15

PIECES OF EIGHT

Serving on the staff of an admiral at sea can have its privileges. Although the weight of Royal Navy tradition is ever present, and despite defence spending cuts and overstretched manpower, when an admiral is at sea in his flagship a hundred years can roll back to mirror a way of life more appropriate to the age when steam replaced sail, rather than the world of satellite navigation systems and laser-guided weapons. One such privilege, in the grand country-house tradition, was breakfast.

This was always served in the admiral's day cabin which in a County-class guided-missile destroyer stretched the width of the ship. Designed personally by Lord Mountbatten to ensure that his admirals should not only have sufficient space in which to conduct the daily business of manoeuvring the ships under their command at sea, but also to provide hospitality in a manner more befitting royalty when in harbour.

Thus it was that the admiral, his chief of staff,

his secretary, his flag lieutenant and one of his staff weapons officers would sit down at the long, highly polished mahogany table and over devilled kidneys, sautéed mushrooms or kedgeree, together with the ubiquitous Frank Cooper's marmalade and Gentleman's Relish, discuss the flotilla's inadequate station-keeping, weapon serviceability or helicopter crew fatigue. In harbour, our routine was more relaxed. Conversation would more likely concentrate on the monumental traffic jam which had prevented prompt arrival at last evening's ambassadorial cocktail party, or why the flagship's guard of honour for a visiting foreign dignitary had paraded on the wrong side of the railway lines on the jetty so that they were completely masked by the unexpected arrival of a train loaded with containers for the Panamanian-registered freighter berthed ahead.

It was against such a harbour background that we took our places one bright autumn morning in Antwerp. With two accompanying frigates we were representing Her Majesty's Government at the city's celebration of its liberation by the Allies some forty years earlier. At breakfast on this occasion we were joined by our liaison officer, a Belgian army major, and the admiral's wife and two children who had arrived the day before by ferry from England.

As many ceremonial and diplomatic events were planned Mrs Admiral had felt she could contribute and assist her husband in the social round. The presence of the children was less easy to reconcile but the visit coincided with half-term holiday from their boarding schools and the admiral's daughter would be ten years old the following day. So breakfast this Saturday morning, despite the silver service and gold braid, was more of a happy family occasion.

After we had finished our fresh grapefruit, the admiral asked his daughter what she would like to do for her birthday tomorrow. The Belgian major answered immediately. 'Vee half already agreed, admiral, that she should wisit the famous Antwerp bird market. It is vell-known all over Europe and people come from hundreds of miles to sell their birds at this market.'

'How marvellous!' said the admiral. 'Sam will love that.'

'Yes,' replied Samantha smiling, her eyes shining, 'Major Albert says I can buy a parrot.'

'Of course you can, my darling,' said the admiral, 'and we will take it back home for you on the ship to Portsmouth.'

Sam's eyes widened. 'Oh, thank you, Daddy. I've always wanted a parrot.'

'That's settled then,' said the admiral. 'Sam and Christopher can go with Major Albert to the bird market. My wife and I will go to the special commemoration service at the cathedral.' The chief steward placed two silver racks with warm toast on the starched linen tablecloth.

Clearing my throat and sitting forward in my chair, I hesitated.

'Yes, Roger?'

'Well, there's just one thing, sir. I have to advise that buying a parrot is not really a very good idea, as we may not be allowed to import it into the UK. There are very strict customs rules about importing birds.'

'Are you saying that Sam can't have her birthday present?' asked the admiral? A frosty silence descended over the breakfast table. The chief steward, standing deferentially behind the admiral's chair, averted his gaze from the breakfast scene and studiously watched the patterns made by the water in the harbour shimmering through the portholes.

'I'm not saying she can't have a parrot,' I replied, 'but we may not be able to land it so she can have it at home in England.'

'Don't be such a mean old spoil sport, Roger,' said Mrs Admiral. 'It's Sam's birthday and she has wanted a parrot for ages, haven't you, sweetheart?'

'Yes,' gulped Sam, her eyes filling with tears. 'I want a parrot for my birthday, I really want a parrot.'

'And so you shall have one,' beamed Major Albert, sensing an uncomfortable diplomatic incident rather than a passing family altercation. 'I shall buy one for you myself and a cage.'

Samantha smiled thinly, sniffed loudly and

wiped her eyes. The admiral glowered and the only sound was the scraping of knives against the now cold toast. The once cheerful family breakfast stumbled to conclusion. We dispersed to our harbour duties.

On Sunday there was great excitement when Major Albert and the children arrived on board with Samantha's birthday parrot squawking and hopping in its cage. I admired its plumage and coloured crest whilst enjoying a slice of Sam's birthday cake. Inwardly, however, my heart sank over what I was sure would be difficulties ahead. The next day we were due to sail for Portsmouth. The admiral's wife and children said their farewells, which included Sam's to her cherished parrot, now happily swinging in its cage from the deckhead in the admiral's day cabin. The admiral transferred to one of the frigates and, to the accompaniment of the local police band, with Major Albert standing to attention and waving from the jetty, the flagship moved slowly out into the River Scheldt.

Whilst the presence of the parrot on board had inevitably caused much ribald comment among the sailors, it had been readily accepted as manifestation of an admiral's eccentricity and in keeping with the best traditions of the senior service. My views were more pragmatic, but whilst the bird was safely caged in the admiral's cabin, shipboard life would continue undisturbed. As soon as we had dropped the pilot the ship began to experience the swell of the North Sea and a strong south-westerly wind. This was in marked contrast to the sheltered waters of the river. With the barometer falling, the admiral decided to delay his return and we settled into an uncomfortable routine ploughing into a Force 6.

The ship heaved and rolled but wedged in my cabin I was able to catch up on some paperwork. A steward knocked on the door. 'I fink you'd better come quick to the admiral's cabin, sir,' he said gloomily. 'It looks to me like 'is parrot's snuffed it!' 'I don't believe it,' I groaned and lurched down to the great cabin. The steward had removed the cage and wedged it on the deck beneath the table. 'Look, Sir, it's been lying like that for about twenty minutes. It don't seem to move at all.' My mind raced. The parrot dead? It had not been on board for more than a day and my concern about facing HM Customs and Excise paled into insignificance when compared with incurring the wrath of the admiral or enduring the distress this premature bereavement would undoubtedly cause his daughter.

The parrot lay supine at the bottom of the cage, its eyes closed. I touched its feathered breast and rolled it over. No movement at all. 'Don't you fink it's dead?' said the steward pointedly. Knowing little about birds, I could only mumble agreement. 'But we could always ask the Commander (E), sir,' he added brightly.

'I know 'e knows about birds 'cos 'is cabin's got books about 'em and 'e keeps a log of any funny ones 'e sees when we're at sea.' 'OK,' I said, 'I'll ask him but you stay here and keep an eye on that parrot.'

An admiral's staff officer at sea is something of a cuckoo in the nest of the ship's own officers, so my request for assistance would not be a formality. There was no time to lose. 'Sorry to disturb you, Engines,' I said, 'but I think the admiral's parrot may have died. I'm told you know about birds and might be able to help.' 'Huh,' he snorted and sucked at his pipe. 'I'm not surprised it's dead. Bloody good job too I'd say, because there's no way HM Customs will allow it into the country and I don't want my shore leave stopped because of some effing parrot.' Whilst these remarks were not wholly helpful, or the sort of diagnosis I had expected, his views mirrored my own. 'All the same, would you have a look at it?' I pleaded, self-preservation overtaking all else. 'All right,' he replied grumpily and together we went to the admiral's quarters.

The steward held open the cage as the Commander (E) expertly lifted out the parrot. He opened each eyelid with his finger. 'Nope, he's not dead. He's just seasick and has fallen off his perch. Not surprising really because it's not aligned properly.' 'What do you mean?' I asked, feeling relief the parrot was not dead; concern that it was apparently only seasick; and renewed foreboding at having to explain to HM Customs why we had purchased a parrot abroad and wished to take it ashore in Portsmouth. 'Easy,' he replied, 'the perch should be fixed athwartships across the cage, not forrard to aft. The parrot needs to sway with the movement of the ship from side to side. If it's not like that he can't get his balance, gets sick and falls off. Simple really.'

I had to agree. 'Shall we try him like that?' he added, lifting out the perch from the bars and refixing it across the cage. 'There we are,' he said, putting back the parrot into the cage, fixing its claws over the wooden perch and resting its head against the bars. After several attempts to prop up the parrot in this fashion had failed, he was able at last to wedge the bird sufficiently firmly to ensure it stayed in an upright position. Then very carefully he lifted up the cage and suspended it again from the deckhead hook.

The movement of the ship immediately started to swing the cage from side to side and after a couple of gentle movements one parrot eye opened. The claws stiffened to get a better grip and slowly, in time with the ship's motion, the parrot began to sway from side to side on his perch. 'Told you so,' said the Commander (E). I expressed relieved and heartfelt thanks, congratulated the steward on this alertness, watched a few more synchronised sways from the parrot and then retreated to my cabin to read the voluminous pages of Customs Regulations regarding the import of birds and livestock into the United Kingdom.

Before our arrival in Portsmouth I signalled our logistic requirements on berthing. These included a request for customs clearance for admiral, staff, officers and ship's company, 'plus admiral's parrot'. This last request was, however, regarded as a practical joke by the shore authorities who, not wishing to appear lacking in a sense of humour, signalled in reply 'Customs clearance arranged. Pieces of eight! Pieces of eight!'

We embarked the customs officers beyond Outer Spit buoy in order to start shore leave immediately we berthed alongside. The autumn sun shone, the flags and pennants blew horizontally in the wind, the boatswain's calls shrilled in salute from the shore training establishments and with due pomp the flagship sailed majestically into the harbour. High on the bridge top the admiral acknowledged the salutes and checked the appearance of the accompanying frigates. Down below in the cabin, I sat with the senior customs officer going through the declaration forms. 'Fine, all in order,' he said, 'except there was some mention of a parrot, although we all knew that was a joke so as soon as we are tied up I'll be getting ashore.' He stopped suddenly and followed my finger pointing to the far corner of the cabin where our admiral's daughter's birthday present was perched serenely in its cage.

'Oh,' he gulped. 'This is going to cause a problem. The admiral won't be able to leave the ship as we haven't made any special arrangements.' Suddenly the noise of the ship's engines ceased and I realised that we were alongside the jetty. Gangways were being lifted on board and preparations made to get the ship into harbour routine.

The admiral came into the cabin bright-eyed and rosy-cheeked. I introduced the customs officer. 'Well,' said the admiral, 'No point in hanging about. I assume, Roger, you've sorted out everything with our customs chap here, so I'll be going.'

'Excuse me, sir, there is just one thing,' said the customs officer to the admiral. 'I'm afraid I shall not be able to allow you ashore until the Ministry of Agriculture and Fisheries inspector has checked your parrot. The regulations regarding bringing birds into the country must be enforced. Parrots in particular. As the owner you are personally responsible.'

The admiral looked at the customs officer, then at me. I was too polite to say, 'I told you so,' but the admiral did it for me.

'That's exactly what this officer told me,' replied the admiral. 'Indeed because the rules are so strict I thought it best if I gave the parrot to him!'

I gasped. Was I hearing this correctly? 'I beg

your pardon, sir,' I spluttered, 'but the parrot was bought for Samantha and therefore it must be yours.'

'Not at all,' replied the admiral, 'you've looked after it. Let me know when everything's fixed so Sam can come down and pick it up. Is that all right, officer?' he added, turning to the astonished customs official.

'Absolutely, sir, if it is not your property I have no right to detain you a moment longer.'

'Grand!' said the admiral and left the cabin. Five minutes later I heard the ship's bugler sound the 'Alert' announcing that the admiral had left the ship.

The customs officer was sympathetic. 'I'll telephone the Ag and Fish office but the nearest one is in Winchester so it'll be a few hours before anyone can come down here. In the meantime, sir, I am very sorry you will not be allowed to go ashore and I cannot sign the declaration form. This will have to be amended to show the parrot is a bird you have purchased outside the UK and wish to bring into this country for your personal use.'

I nodded dumbly in agreement.

Later that same afternoon a harassed ministry inspector, conspicuous in trilby and country tweeds, arrived. Having driven thirty miles to answer an emergency call to inspect a parrot belonging to an admiral on board a RN warship he was not in the best of humour. I showed him the bird.

CALL THE HANDS

'That's not a parrot,' he said, scowling. 'That's a cockatiel. Why did you say it was a parrot?' I did not have the energy to explain that this 'cockatiel' did not even belong to me. 'Still, as it's a cockatiel,' he continued, 'the rules are more straightforward. If you are prepared to sign these declarations about its future habitat and caging, it can be removed from the ship after seven days.' At that point I would have signed anything concerning parrots, cockatiels or even albatrosses, as long as I was not going to be put in quarantine as well.

I telephoned the admiral at home. 'Marvellous news, Roger. I knew you'd sort it out. We'll all come down to Portsmouth next week to collect it. Sam will be over the moon.'

With the forms duly signed and as soon as the inspector had left the ship I sent for the duty midshipman. 'That is a bird,' I said slowly, pointing to the cage containing the cockatiel, 'belonging to the admiral. It is extremely valuable so guard it with your life. When you hand over to your relief tomorrow, tell him the same. In seven days time the admiral will return to collect it. Make sure it is fed and watered. And alive. If it is not, neither will you be!' 'Aye aye, sir,' replied the young man, visibly shaken. He knew I was not joking.

16

FORE!

When I was appointed to the staff of the Captain Fishery Protection Squadron based at South Queensferry near Edinburgh in Scotland, my father, in view of the location of my new posting, felt it was the ideal time to give me his golf clubs. He had reached the stage where he believed the person who described golf as 'a long walk spoilt' was correct. He had taken up playing bowls instead.

The taxi from Edinburgh Waverley station took me to the minesweeper base located on the south bank of the River Forth in the shadow of the mighty railway bridge. As we pulled up outside the small wardroom mess the hall porter, realising that a new officer had arrived, came out to help. 'I'll take these, sir,' he said in a strong Scottish accent, indicating my bags and suitcases. 'You'll be wanting to carry yon clubs yerself!' Swinging my golf bag nonchantly over my shoulder, in the manner I had seen golfers do, although I had never even held a club let alone tried to hit a golf ball, I paid off the taxi and followed the porter towards the doors into the mess.

These were double plate-glass doors and with my briefcase in one hand and my golf clubs over my shoulder I was not used to negotiating such entrances. With my free hand and shoulder I pushed myself awkwardly through the doors and into the hallway. As I looked around for the porter one of the glass doors swung back and hit an unprotected steel club head protruding from my bag. With a sound like a thunderclap the glass door disintegrated into a thousand pieces leaving only the frame and some ugly jagged shards! I stood aghast and unable to move.

Immediately the old retainer reappeared and, despite my repeated apologies, he waved them away, saying, 'Och, dinna worry yerself, sir, that was yer golf clubs that did it so it's nae a problem.' I agreed it was my clubs that did the actual damage but it was my own clumsiness which was to blame. Despite my protestations the porter was adamant. 'The Commander,' he whispered conspiratorially, referring to the president of the wardroom mess, 'will nae worry aboot it when he knows you're a golfer!' 'But I'm not a golfer!' I spluttered helplessly. 'Aye, sir,' he replied, giving me a broad wink, 'that's what they all say!'

Later that day, over drinks before dinner, I introduced myself to the Commander as the newly arrived officer who had shattered the door

FORE!

to the mess and offered my abject apologies and willingness to pay for the repairs. But the hall porter was correct. The Commander waved away all my despairing attempts to shoulder the blame, insisting, 'As you're a golfer, Roger, we'll turn a blind eye to the damage. The mess could do with another golfer anyway for we play society matches here nearly every week and as you've got your own clubs we could use your experience.'

It did not seem an appropriate moment to tell him that I'd never played the game in my life, nor even when he added, 'Hope you'll be able to turn out next Wednesday when we play the Edinburgh Merchants. We want to put out a strong team.' Instead I mumbled my thanks for taking such a lenient attitude over the damage to the door and for his generosity in including me in the team. 'No worries,' he said. 'Welcome to Scotland.' It was at that moment that I realised that golf in Scotland stands alongside religion in defining the sort of life you lead. My father's views would have branded him a heretic.

During the next few days I received a comprehensive briefing from the officer I was taking over from and all thoughts of golf were put out of my head. Except when he commented, 'You'll soon settle in here. Especially as I understand you're a golfer.' He accentuated the last word and smiled knowingly. There was nothing I could say as I knew by now that 'I'm not really a golfer' was always regarded as total humbug and a classic example of every golfer's assumed modesty. That it happened to be the truth in my case was irrelevant. Even when I met other golfers who as soon as they knew I was 'the man who smashed the door with his golf clubs' would ask, 'What do you play off then?' My nervous laugh in reply was always treated with 'heard it all before' disdain.

Arrangements for the match the following week were published and my selection for the team confirmed. Not having my own transport to get to the course it was decided that I should accompany the captain of the base, himself a keen golfer, in his official limousine. Just before lunch on Wednesday, however, I was given a message: 'The captain sends his apologies but he is now unable to play golf this afternoon but still wants you to use his official car to get to the golf course. It will then return to wait for him at the meeting which has necessitated him withdrawing from the golf match.' It all seemed extremely complicated to me and I would have much preferred to have been told simply that I was not now playing.

But it was not to be. Promptly at 1 p.m. Captain Fishery Protection's official black Daimler with uniformed chauffeur pulled up outside the wardroom mess. To add to my embarrassment the chauffeur insisted on carrying my clubs – my father's old hand-me-downs – to the car and reverently placing them in the boot before holding open the door so that I could sit in polished luxury in the rear. As we drove imperiously through the base I received many smart salutes as officers and sailors recognised 'CFP's limo'. My concern at being exposed as a golfing imposter was compounded when I realised that I could now also be accused of impersonating a senior officer!

A secluded private road led through the magnificently landscaped parkland golf course to the former stately mansion which was now the clubhouse. As the road wound its way past wide fairways and manicured greens the Daimler slowed to a suitably sedate pace. Overwhelmed with a sense of utter inadequacy, I shrank further into the leather upholstery. With a heavy crunching of gravel the car came to a halt outside the doric-columned entrance. My driver held open the door and carefully handed over my clubs. 'Enjoy your game, sir,' he said, touching his cap. 'The captain will be sorry not to be playing with you.' I smiled politely but muttered to myself, 'He won't when he hears how bad I am!'

Left on my own I looked around. The only thing to do, I decided, was to act like a golfer. But never having been to a golf club before I did not really know what this entailed. I went up the steps to the main entrance. 'No Golf Clubs allowed in the Clubhouse' a notice informed me. I carefully propped my golf bag against the wall, thankful that negotiating the imposing-looking door with my clubs over my shoulder would not, on this occasion, be necessary.

Inside the vestibule sat a smartly uniformed attendant. I took a deep breath. 'I'm here to play golf,' I announced, 'for the Navy against the Edinburgh Merchants.' He looked down at a list on his desk. 'Aye, Sir, that's right. They're teeing off at two o'clock. You'll want to get yourself changed.' He could sense my puzzlement at this last remark and added, 'In the gentlemen's changing room, sir. You go out of the front door and around the side to the right.'

I thanked him and left to follow his instructions. But as I walked down the wide stone steps I wondered what on earth he could mean by 'get yourself changed'. To me 'changed' indicated that one had something to 'change' into. For all the other sports I had played, such as rugby where you changed into your team's colours and studded boots, or cricket with white flannels and a sweater, I would have been prepared. But whatever clothing it was I was supposed to have to 'change' into to play golf, I certainly did not have it with me!

I pushed open the door marked 'Gentlemen's Changing' and went inside. Fortunately there were a few familiar faces. 'Ah, there you are, Roger!' said one, 'Glad you could make it. Better get yourself changed!' Amidst the lockers and benches the others made space for me whilst laughing and chattering amongst themselves.

FORE!

Having served in small ships at sea I was well used to being in close proximity to men either naked or in various stages of undress, but I also knew it was not a good idea to stare too long or directly at them as they took off their trousers and shirts, which my fellow golfers were doing.

My interest though was not in what they were taking off but what they would be putting on to play golf. It slowly become apparent that a golfer's playing 'kit' was a sort of designer leisurewear that could just as easily be worn off, as on, a golf course. I felt hugely relieved at this discovery and that I was, after all, not going to be overtly conspicuous or improperly attired.

Accordingly I took off my blazer and tie and hung them on a hook. I then opened the top button of my shirt. In an instant, it appeared, I was ready. I did not look much different from some of my companions who were taking considerably longer with their own changing. But not wishing to appear too keen, I busied myself by rehanging my jacket at couple of times, taking off my trousers then putting them back on again, and smoothing out, at length, my tie. It was a complete charade intended solely to give the appearance of 'changing' and to divert any undue attention away from the simple fact that I was not a golfer and had no proper golfing clothes.

More difficult was the matter of footwear. I watched my fellow players as they took off the shoes they had arrived in and put on special golfing shoes which were spiked and sometimes two-toned with floppy leather tongues. There seemed to be only one thing for me to do in case anyone was watching. I took off the shoes I was wearing – fortunately brown brogues – stared at them hard for a minute or two, fiddled with the laces, and then put them back on again. At last I felt confident enough to stand up. 'All set, Roge?' asked our team captain. 'We're playing fourballs and you're paired with Jim here!' 'Good,' I replied, not understanding a word of what he said but shaking Jim's hand firmly as he introduced himself.

We made our way to the first tee where everyone was gathering. Fortunately we were drawn in the last group to start. I followed my companions to the practice putting green. This was more like it, I thought. Putting should not be a problem and perhaps, after all, this game of golf would turn out to be less intimidating than I had imagined. Memories of seaside holidays with 'clock golf' or pitch and putt on the promenade links came flooding back. Golf on the course where I now found myself was probably nothing more than a grown-up version of these games. No different from going from a football kick-about in the park to playing in a refereed game with eleven players on both sides on a proper pitch. What had I been so worried about?

It was time for our foursome to tee off. 'The

first is a par 4, dog leg to the left,' said my playing partner. I nodded. It was all total gobbledegook to me but there was no turning back. I watched the other players closely – how they placed their ball, which club they selected, and how they swung the club back over their shoulder. Now it was my turn. Do exactly the same as they've done, I repeated over and over again to myself as I placed my ball carefully on the peg tee. I looked down, momentarily thinking that even my brown brogues did not look too much out of place, drew back my driver and swung it down on the small white ball. There was a satisfactory 'ping' and the ball flew high and straight down the middle of the fairway, clearing bunkers and landing more than 200 yards away. 'Shot!' said the others. 'You wee bugger!' said my teammate, 'an I thought you said you couldna play golf!'

It was very soon obvious that I couldn't. I went round in 153.

17

CHRISTMAS AT SEA

Robert Louis Stevenson's evocative poem 'Christmas at Sea' symbolises the tough life in a sailing ship:

The sheets were frozen hard, and they cut the naked hand;
The decks were like a slide, where a seaman scarce could stand;
The wind was a nor'wester, blowing squally off the sea;
And cliffs and spouting breakers were the only things a-lee.

Traditionally, Christmas is a time for getting together at home with family, friends and loved ones. To enjoy the timeless trappings of turkey, mince pies, lights on the tree, decorations, presents, pantomimes and parties. But for those at sea in the Royal Navy, Christmas is a time which often means working on board, frequently far away from home. Much is done, however, to make it seem like being at home.

This may not always be easy, but sailors have never lacked imagination and resourcefulness. On 25 December 1867, HMS *Galatea* was visiting Melbourne, Australia. The Captain recorded:

Numbers of people came off to see the ship; and were much interested in seeing the way the men had decorated their mess-places with all kinds of paper ornaments manufactured by themselves, and quantities of green branches of trees, bearing the nearest resemblance they could find to the Christmas decorations in use at home.

Attempting to enjoy Christmas in the same way as at home remains the underlying theme. In the Royal Navy a Christmas tree used to be hoisted to the top of the mainmast as the ship's own yuletide decoration. In Grand Harbour Malta, fifty years ago, RN ships would have represented a small forest of fir. Today it is more likely ships will be illuminated with floodlights or a necklace of lights from bow to stern.

In 230 ports worldwide the Mission to Seafarers, part of the Anglican Church, cares for seafarers of all nationalities and faiths. At Christmas, its Seafarers Centres are decorated for the occasion, special services and carol singing are organised and entertainment and festive food prepared. In Hong Kong the mission often hands out nearly 4,000 presents to seafarers and in home ports it is not unusual for over 500 presents to be given to seafarers during the Christmas period.

In a warship on Christmas Day, the crew's quarters will be visited by the ship's captain, traditionally accompanied by the youngest sailor on board. In the days of rum issue the captain would have been offered a 'Christmas tot'. This was always politely refused, for if accepted it is doubtful whether the 'skipper's rounds' would ever have been completed! Nevertheless, ships' Christmas puddings have traditionally contained a generous amount of rum. Another long-held tradition requires the rum, which now has to be purchased ashore, to be poured into the pudding mix by the captain, whilst the ingredients are stirred into a large tub with a boat paddle.

As well as rum-flavoured puddings and cakes (see the recipe at the end of the chapter), Christmas fare enjoyed by sailors has rarely been lacking. Samuel Pepys, when Secretary of the Navy in the seventeenth century, wrote, 'Englishmen, and more especially seamen, love their bellies above everything else.' The meals enjoyed by Aubrey and Maturin in the Patrick O'Brian novels provide a glimpse of what might have been on the table in those days. Not least in *The Yellow Admiral* when 'the porpoises rather strangely jointed by the ship's butcher were served out for Christmas dinner and declared better, far better, than roast pork.'

Two hundred years later a menu from the

aircraft carrier HMS *Hermes*, at sea in the Persian Gulf, shows that nearly 50 separate dishes were available at the four meals served to the 1,800 crew on Christmas Day.

Other traditional events feature on board ships at Christmas. Before satellite links, videos and emails, a concert, or music from the ship's band to accompany carol singing, were popular. Ship's pantomimes, colloquially known in the Royal Navy as 'Sods Operas' ('Sods' being the Ship's Operatic and Dramatic Society), are often enjoyed. Like the traditional ceremony of 'Crossing the Line', held when a ship crosses the Equator, pantomimes give the crew an opportunity to dress up as outlandish characters in bizarre costumes. Although scripts are full of bawdy humour they keep to recognised stories. The pantomime *Dick Whittington* was performed on board HMS *Endurance* patrolling the frozen seas of Antarctica. The opening chorus contained the appropriate words 'But if you don't like it, or it's not nice; Then come back next year, we're doing it – on ice!'

Bells, in spite of their association with Christmas decorations, have a more important use on board ship. Striking the ship's bell denotes the passing of time and signifies when watches are due to change. At midnight 'eight bells' is struck, except at midnight on New Year's Eve when the number is doubled to 'sixteen bells'. On this occasion, 'eight bells' is struck for the Old Year, followed immediately by a further 'eight bells' for the New.

For those spending Christmas at sea it will never be exactly the same as at home. Yet thanks to some long-held traditions, and the generosity of those who contribute to making the lives of seafarers more comfortable, the festive season for sailors is still a time to be enjoyed, and remembered.

> *And well I knew the talk they had, the talk that was of me,*
> *Of the shadow on the household and the son that went to sea:*
> *And O the wicked fool I seemed, in every kind of way,*
> *To be here and hauling frozen ropes on blessed Christmas Day.*

CALL THE HANDS

Recipe for Christmas Rum Cake

Ingredients

8 oz (225 gm) butter	8 oz (225 gm) soft brown sugar
4 eggs	10 oz (275 gm) plain white flour
2½ lbs (1.2 kg) raisins	6 fluid oz (150 ml) Pusser's Rum

4 oz (100 gm) flaked almonds 1 heaped teaspoon mixed spice

Method

The day before making the cake put all fruit in a deep bowl and pour over the rum. Cover and leave to soak overnight. Use greased and lined 7"-square, 3"-deep cake tin.

Cream butter and sugar in a very large bowl until light and fluffy. Beat eggs and add to the creamed mixture a little at a time, beating well as you go. Mix flour and spice and fold in with a metal spoon. Add soaked fruit and nuts and any remaining rum. Mix well, turn into the cake tin.

Bake in a pre-heated oven 150°C (300°F) Gas Mark 2, for approximately 2½ hours. Check after 2 hours and if cake is dark enough in colour cover with greaseproof paper. To test if cake is fully cooked pierce with a fine skewer. If the skewer comes out clean, the cake is cooked. Cool in the tin. Remove and wrap in greaseproof paper before storing in a cake tin.

18

TELL ME ABOUT YOURSELF

Seeking employment after a career as a service officer is a major challenge. You will not get that civilian job, or any sort of appointment, without meeting with your potential employer, an agency, a head hunter, or a human-resources specialist. Indeed, the whole effort of a job search campaign is geared towards obtaining that all-important interview. It is the one stage of the entire process where you will be on your own. Where you alone can succeed or fail. Or is it?

Like many others before me, I made the mistake of assuming that interviewers knew what sort of person they wanted, would conduct the interview along the lines I had been told to expect, and would ask questions in accordance with the perceived wisdom of countless counsellors. So it always seemed rather unfair when I had produced a finely tuned CV, meticulously completed every question on the application form, obtained as much background information as I could about the firm, memorised the questions I would like to ask, spent time on reconnaissance, arrived ten minutes early in a smart business suit, sober tie and polished shoes, and practised the answers to the three inevitable questions: 'What sort of job are you looking for?', 'Why did you leave the Royal Navy?' and 'Tell me about yourself?', only to find myself being interviewed in a manner no amount of training and study could ever have prepared me for!

The offices were open-plan with potted plants in profusion. The receptionist's gloss-lipstick smile, as she handed me a cup of fresh-ground coffee, augured well. Fifteen minutes after the time arranged for interview, I enquired whether Mr Smythe, with whom I had the appointment, knew I had arrived. 'Oh sure,' she cooed. Open-neck shirted and designer-jeaned executives swished past, snippets of conversation about drawings and deadlines buzzed in my ears. I looked through the *Architects' Journal* and read the testimonials to the firm's work framed on the walls.

'Certainly, Mr Smythe. At once, Mr Smythe,' I heard Gloss Lips say and awoke from my reverie of absorbing the culture of the firm to see a tall figure pacing away from reception. 'That,' she said helpfully but a trifle obviously, 'was Mr Smythe,' and before I could ask, added 'He does know you're here.' Some twenty minutes later and determined not to be caught napping again, I saw the same figure I now knew to be Mr

TELL ME ABOUT YOURSELF

Smythe, returning. I decided to introduce myself. 'Hello,' I said, standing up as he was about to walk past, 'I'm Mr Paine, here to be interviewed for the post of practice administrator.' 'Good,' he said. 'Have a seat will you? I'll be right back,' and disappeared behind some partitions.

I sat down, deflated. Gloss Lips smiled sweetly and offered another coffee which I grumpily refused. Time ticked away until Mr Smythe at last reappeared. 'Now then Mr ... er ... er... What did you say your name was again?' I told him. 'Let's try and find somewhere we can have a chat although I haven't got much time today as I'm off to Ascot.' He indicated his striped trousers and grey waistcoat. I experienced a strong feeling that my interview for the post of practice administrator was probably not high on Mr Smythe's list of priorities.

Having found an empty room, after two attempts to interrupt meetings in others had failed, we sat down. He shuffled a folder of papers, desperately hunting for my application. 'Ah, here we are,' he announced. I hoped he was looking at the right one. 'Now you've seen the job description, is there anything you would like to know?' 'I was wondering,' I replied, 'although I can see the offices are mainly open-plan, whether I would have my own separate office?' 'Ummm,' he mused, it was clearly something which he had not considered. 'Good question, but as you would be in charge of accommodation, perhaps that would be your first task!' He chuckled loudly at this spontaneous and witty reply. I smiled in response, but with less enthusiasm. 'If that were to be the case,' I replied, 'would you be able to give me some indication of where I should start looking?' Having parried my first unexpected question, he was clearly puzzled that I should continue. After a few moments his face brightened. 'I know,' he said, grinning broadly, 'There's always been an old desk and chair in the basement, so you might start there!' I had to assume he was joking, so I laughed too.

Suddenly there was a loud knock on the door. A man in blue overalls stood in the doorway. 'You all gotta get aht!' he shouted. Mr Smythe and I looked around in surprise. 'You all gotta get aht!' he repeated. 'Fire exercise. Everybody's gotta get aht!' Without waiting for our reaction, he moved on down the corridor where he could be heard intoning 'You all gotta get aht!' at other occupants. Mr Smythe turned. 'I think we've got to get out. Fire exercise.' 'Yes,' I said, 'that seemed to be the message.' There was no time for further discussion and the one-o'clock race forty miles away was coming up fast, so we went down the stairs together and out onto the street. 'I'll let you know,' said Mr Smythe. The interview was over. I didn't get the job.

The firm of Mayfair solicitors had three long-deceased partners' names on the brass plate outside their marble-columned offices and an awesome air of respectability. Maroon Wilton carpet, prints of old London, and sepia photographs of stiff-collared, bewhiskered partners stared accusingly down. It was my second interview, as I had successfully hurdled the no-nonsense HR officer at my first.

Four partners sat facing me across the leather-bound boardroom table. My homework this time had not been in vain. Questioning was rigorous but fair. It came to the last partner's turn. Looking down at my CV and over his half-moons he said, 'I see amongst your leisure activities you are interested in amateur dramatics, but you were in the Royal Navy. What opportunities did you get for amateur dramatics there?' 'When we were ashore,' I countered, 'we often used to put on plays and each year there was a RN Drama Festival which I was involved with from time to time.' 'Yes,' he continued, 'but what about when you were at sea?' 'There would sometimes be pantomimes at Christmas, or the ceremony for Crossing the Line,' I replied.

This aspect of my career was interesting him greatly, although it seemed less relevant to me. 'But did you dress up?' he persisted. 'Well, yes, people did dress up,' I said. 'But did *you* dress up?' He accented the word 'you'. The implications were obvious. 'I did sometimes, though usually I wrote or produced the play or show,' I said. 'Did people dress up as women?' He was not going to give up. 'Yes,' I admitted, 'you would get some guys dressing up as women.' 'Did you?' A lawyer's questions are not easily avoided. 'No, I did not,' I said. 'So what was it you dressed up for? Was it skits, concert parties or what?' he asked, staring hard. He reminded me of a dog who had buried a bone and was just about to unearth it. Exasperated by this cross-examination, I felt I had no option but to admit, 'If you really must know, we used to call them "Sods Operas".' 'No further questions,' he said, taking off his glasses. The interview was over. I didn't get that job either.

The chartered accountancy partnership was less intimidating. Mr Barratt, the senior partner, was bluff and cheerfully admitted he couldn't remember my name 'or anyone else's in the firm until they've been here twenty years'. My first interview focused on what I enjoyed doing most after work and at weekends. Having established that I played sport, he raised the all-important question of what I did to relax afterwards. 'Do you drink?' 'Yes, I like a drink.' 'What do you drink?' 'Usually beer,' I said. 'What sort of beer?' he asked. 'Bitter or Guinness.' 'What sort of bitter?' I replied that I had no particular favourites. 'Do you like Greene King?' 'Yes, that's a really good pint.' The senior partner's eyes lit up and we spent the next hour chatting about the various merits of Theakston's, Marston's, Friary Meux, Breakspear's, Adnam's and other well-known real ales. The relevance of this whirlwind tour of traditional breweries to a new appointment in a firm of accountants escaped me, although I found out afterwards that if I had said I drank lager the interview would have been terminated at that point. My interview self-assessment, as I had been trained to undertake, was unusually difficult.

Two weeks passed and I had heard nothing. With some trepidation and, assuming that the appointment had been filled, I telephoned. 'No,' said Mr Barratt, 'no decision has yet been made but would you like to come to lunch?' Lunch to the hearty patriarch was the event of the day. We marched into a City wine bar, with considerable deference were shown to a secluded table and were into our tumblers of amontillado before his bowler hat had been taken downstairs to its own hidden peg. He introduced me to the waitresses, advised me always to choose one of the 'specials' and negotiated a substantial discount on a bottle of Château Ausone 1982, before launching into an amusing flow of stories, several of them concerning his experience as a navigator in the RAF during World War II.

I was still hoping for some mention of the post when he enquired, 'Would you like a port with your Stilton before we go back and see if you want the job?' Trying to remain calm and sober and remember the preparations I had made to get this far, I declined. 'Huh,' he snorted, 'I thought all Royal Navy officers drank port, but if you won't join me I'll have one myself.' I realised at once I had made a serious error and said that, after all, I would. He beamed. 'That's more like it, we'll have two large vintage Warre's. They keep it very well here.' He continued to reminisce, ordering two further glasses, until at about 4.15 p.m. we made our way, somewhat unsteadily, back to his office. He shook hands outside. 'No point in coming in now. Far too late. Will be in touch.' My second interview was over.

Another two weeks passed before I felt confident enough to telephone again and enquire if I had, after our last meeting, been lucky enough to secure the job. 'Good heavens, no!' chuckled Mr Barratt. 'But I did enjoy our lunch! So I think you should now meet the other partners, over lunch.' Did this mean I had to face seventeen gastronomic marathons for which the first had been only a warm-up? I was reassured that it would be lunch with all of them together at the firm's head office in a week's time.

We assembled in the boardroom. The partners introduced themselves over pre-lunch drinks. A grey-haired gentleman approached. 'I hear you used to be in the Royal Navy,' he smiled encouragingly. 'I did my National Service in the Royal Air Force.' Without a second thought, I gave the standard knee-jerk reply ingrained into every officer of the other two services, 'Well, we all go through life with a cross to bear!' The smile left his face and he moved away extremely crestfallen. Immediately I realised my mistake. This conversation was really part of my job interview. I wished the floor could open up. What had I done?

But I did get that job, although there was one partner who never again mentioned his Service career. Or mine.

19

THE SHIP'S WAKE

Stand at the stern rail and watch the ship's wake,
It bubbles and tumbles like water in a washing machine,
But wakes bubbled and tumbled long before convenience appliances,
Vasco da Gama, Magellan, Columbus and Cook watched the ship's wake.

Stand at the stern rail and watch the ship's wake,
Stencilling the passage of a ship through the sea,
Marking the time and the speed and the distance,
Immeasurable in itself, yet an immemorial measure of time.

Stand at the stern rail and watch the ship's wake,
Look into the churning foam or the slowly stretching ripples,
The sea opens, is disturbed and closes again,
The wake is a signature in the sea that a ship has passed this way.

CALL THE HANDS

Stand at the stern rail and watch the ship's wake,
Traditionally white but always reflecting the water it leaves behind;
Cobalt blue Atlantic troughs, iridescent Mediterranean chops,
Ochre Ganges silt and scum swilling out into the Indian Ocean.

Stand at the stern rail and watch the ship's wake,
Stirring the water below, bringing to the surface food from the ocean's floor
Or the galley's gash, slung into the chute by a cook going off watch,
For gulls, terns, skuas and Mother Carey's chickens who swoop, soar and swallow.

Stand at the stern rail and watch the ship's wake,
By night phosphorous without a moon, shimmering ethereal in the moonlight,
By day flashing brief rainbows, as the sea's spray filters the sunlight,
What matter created by turbines, generators, diesel motors, shafts and propellors.

A wake can stretch to the horizon, straight as a narrow road across the polders
But bent as a dog's hind leg when a novice helmsman is 'getting the feel';
It mesmerises, tranquilises, energises, and satisfies that we're moving on,
Stand at the stern rail and watch the ship's wake.